TITLE SEARCHING IN ONTARIO

Third Edition

TITLE SEARCHING IN ONTARIO
A Procedural Guide

Third Edition

Janet M. Globe

Butterworths
Toronto   Vancouver

Title Searching in Ontario
© 1991 Butterworths Canada Ltd.

Printed and bound in Canada

The Butterworth Group of Companies

Canada
    Butterworths Canada Ltd., 75 Clegg Road, MARKHAM, Ont. L6G 1A1 and
    409 Granville Street, Suite 1455, VANCOUVER, B.C. V6C 1T2
Australia
    Butterworths Pty Ltd., SYDNEY, MELBOURNE, BRISBANE, ADELAIDE,
    PERTH, CANBERRA and HOBART
Ireland
    Butterworth (Ireland) Ltd., DUBLIN
New Zealand
    Butterworths of New Zealand Ltd., WELLINGTON and AUCKLAND
Puerto Rico
    Equity de Puerto Rico, Inc., HATO REY
Singapore
    Malayan Law Journal Pte. Ltd., SINGAPORE
United Kingdom
    Butterworth & Co. (Publishers) Ltd., LONDON and EDINBURGH
United States
    Butterworth Legal Publishers, AUSTIN, Texas; BOSTON, Massachusetts;
    CLEARWATER, Florida (D & S Publishers); ORFORD, New Hampshire
    (Equity Publishing); ST. PAUL, Minnesota; and SEATTLE, Washington.

Canadian Cataloguing in Publication Data

Globe, Janet M.
  Title searching in Ontario

3rd ed.
Includes index.
ISBN 0-409-89382-X

1. Title examinations — Ontario.   2. Land titles —
Ontario.   I. Title.

KE0274.G56 1991   346.71304'38   C91-093329-4

Sponsoring editor: Charmian Harvey
Editor: Anne Lynas Shah
Cover design: Brant Cowie
Production: Kevin Skinner

To

M.E.T. Payne, B.A., LL.B. for his invaluable assistance
in research and legal opinion.

and to

The title searchers and friends for their assistance,
motivation and support.

PREFACE

This procedural guide has been designed to assist students in understanding the complex subject of title searching. It summarizes the operational framework, and provides direction to the corresponding legislation introduced under the Acts relating to land transactions in Ontario.

It is not a legal publication, so for legal opinion the reader should consult a solicitor.

Janet M. Globe
September 29, 1990
Toronto, Ontario

CONTENTS

PART II   THE LAND TITLES ACT

PART III   THE CONDOMINIUM ACT

PART IV   CLOSINGS

PART V   THE LAND REGISTRATION REFORM ACT, 1984

APPENDICES

HISTORY

Title to the land incorporating the Province of Ontario was claimed by the Crown in the right of Canada. Settlers who arrived in the late eighteenth century were issued Crown Patents by the province under the Crown Lands Act.

The Registry Act, enacted in 1795, provided legislation to introduce public notice pertaining to land records and, in accordance with the Act, land registration offices were organized in a number of districts of northern Ontario and in the southern counties. Crown Patents were registered and the first land registration offices began to function.

In 1885, the Land Titles system was legislated and, as a result, land registration offices increased throughout the province. Development expanded, and with it administration, so it became necessary to divide large counties into two ridings, with an office in each riding.

Unprecedented growth in land transactions in the 1950s and 1960s, and the failure of land registration offices to keep up with technology, resulted in limited access to the records. Therefore, the provincial government undertook a study of the operation of the two systems and enlisted the Ontario Law Reform Commission to recommend changes.

In 1971, a completely revamped, automated system, the Province of Ontario Land Registration System, POLARIS, was created. POLARIS is no longer just a name. Following a pilot project in 1984 at the Oxford County Registry Office at Woodstock, a province-wide implementation was launched.

The Land Registration Reform Act, 1984, S.O. 1984, c. 32 (L.R.R.A., 1984) was enacted to facilitate introduction to new document forms and a computerized version of the abstract books and parcel register recordings. Further amendments will be legislated under Part III of the Act in the near future.

In the meantime, the function of the original systems will be maintained until completion of the merging with POLARIS.

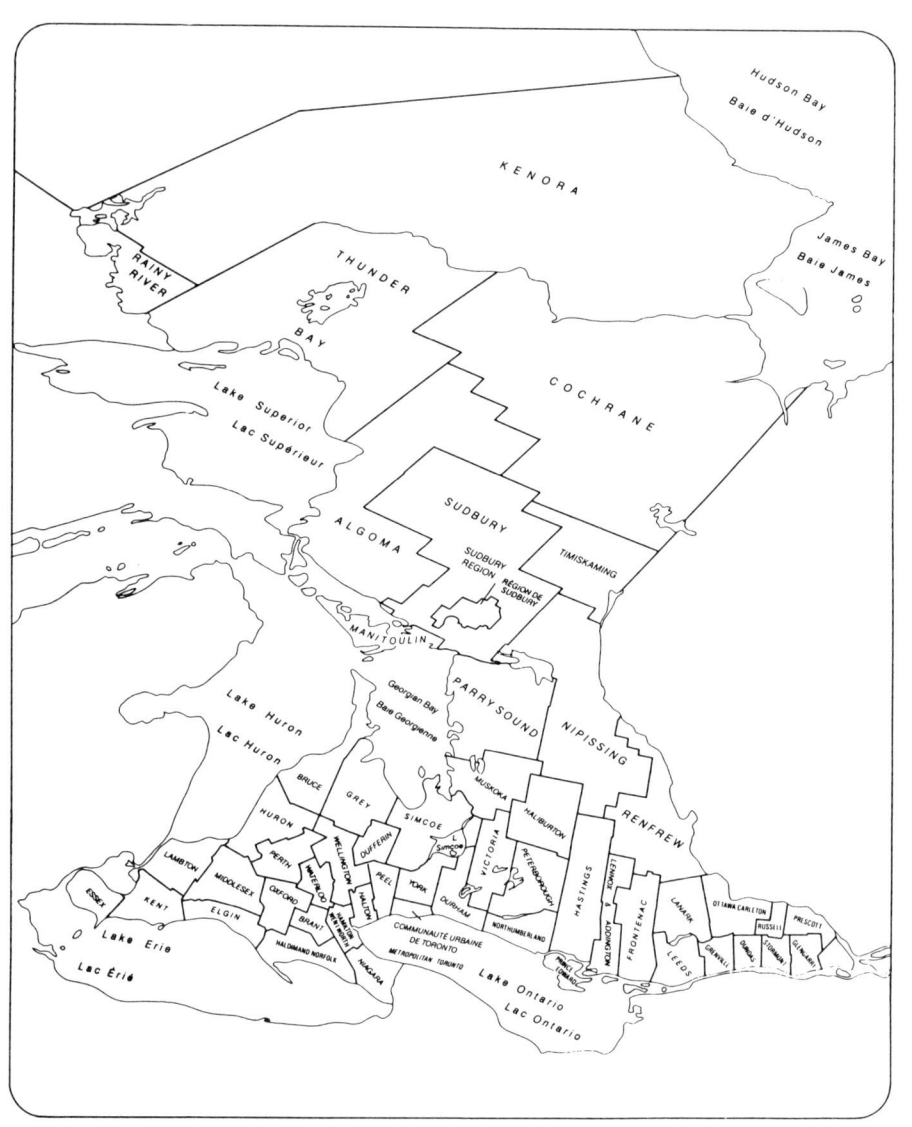

THE PROVINCE OF ONTARIO

IN COUNTIES, DISTRICTS,
REGIONAL AND DISTRICT MUNICIPALITIES

CHAPTER 1

LAND DIVISION IN ONTARIO

During the late eighteenth century the southern part of Ontario was divided into 26 counties and the northern part into 10 districts. The counties were divided into townships, and subsequently Crown surveyors divided the townships into concessions, with lots on the concessions referred to as township lots. On surveys, the lots were numbered with Arabic figures and the concessions identified by Roman numerals.

Initially, surveyors used the Gunter's chain for measuring the lots. One chain measures 66 feet and was divided into 100 links. Acreage was established by multiplying the depth of the lot by the breadth in chains and dividing by 10 (10 square chains = 1 acre). Subsequently, the system of measurement for length and area, the system we are most familiar with, imperial units (feet and inches), was introduced. Finally, Canada committed itself to the metric system on May 25, 1972. Land registrars have accepted land descriptions and plans expressed in imperial or metric units since July 15, 1967.

A road allowance, generally 1 chain (66 feet) in width, separates the concessions, and usually every five township lots. The width varies however, as some allowances are only 40 feet wide. Whether opened or not, the freehold in such allowances vested in the particular municipality by statute, the Municipal Act, R.S.O. 1980, c. 302. Some have never been opened and as a result they have been considered to be part of the township lot.

The Survey Act [now the Surveys Act, R.S.O. 1980, c. 493] describes the seven types of township surveys and provides sketches of the various survey methods. They are too extensive to be discussed in this book, therefore I shall describe only two that have fairly standard dimensions:

(1) a lot 20 chains (1320 feet) wide by 100 chains (6600 feet) deep contains 200 acres. This lot is described as a single front township. The first surveys of such lots were made in 1783 (see below).

(2) a lot 50 chains (3300 feet) wide by 20 chains (1320 feet) deep contains 100 acres. It is described as a front and rear township lot (page 5), the first surveys of which were made in 1787.

Single Front Township Showing Broken Front Lots

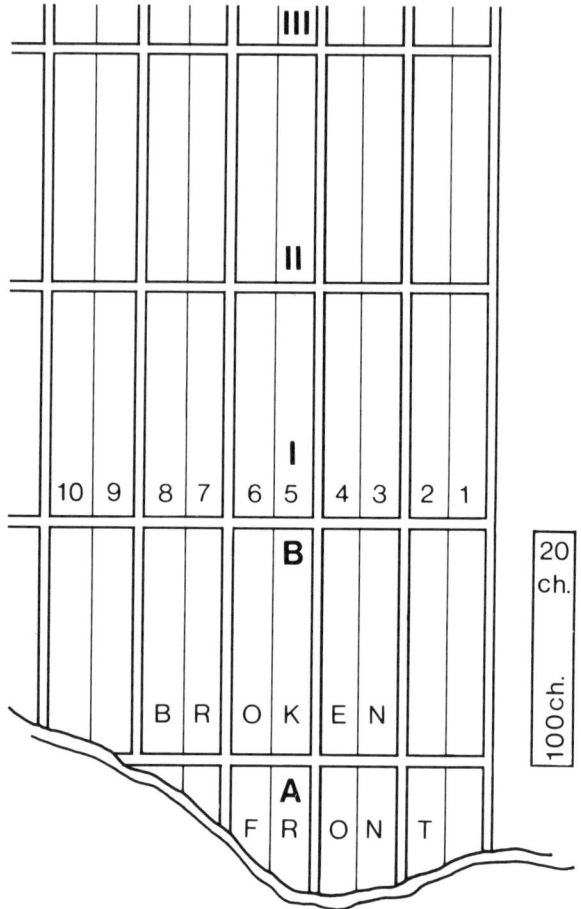

Many township lots have irregular boundaries, *i.e.*, gore lots, which occur when the boundaries are not at right angles to each other and there is a gore with the adjoining township. Shore lines of lakes, rivers and swamps form irregular boundaries and are known as broken front concessions (see above).

Front and Rear Township

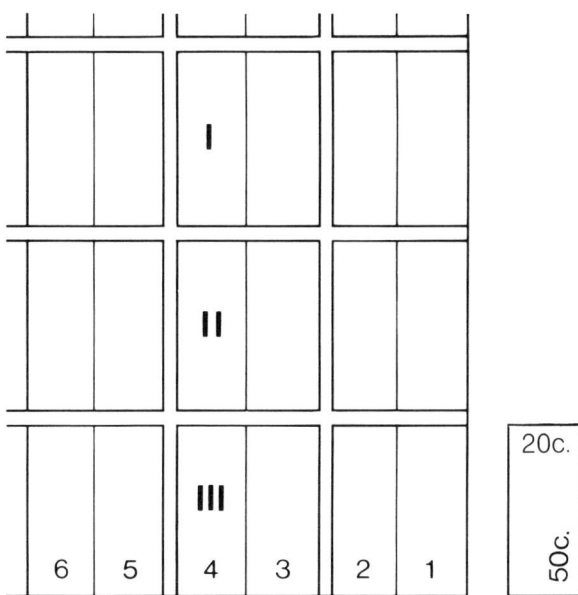

Other types of surveys have caused endless confusion for succeeding generations. One example is the upper part of the Grand River which was settled by ethnic groups. One block, referred to as the German Company Tract, was divided into lots each containing 448 acres. Road allowances were disregarded and so a complex system of roads developed which resulted in many boundary disputes before public roads could be built.

As the population of the province increased the township lots were subdivided into smaller lots which were surveyed and shown on a registered plan. However, the plan system was not regulated so the plans were not always clearly identified.

By the twentieth century control of plan registration became necessary. Such control came by way of the Planning Act in 1946 and, in accordance with this legislation, division of land could occur only by registered plan of subdivision unless a consent to severance pursuant to the provisions of the Planning Act was obtained. Many mistakes were made in the original surveys because of the rugged character of the land, necessitating new surveys as time went on.

The original Crown survey plans of the township lots are available for inspection in the appropriate Registry Office and at the Ministry of Natural Resources, Parliament Buildings: Whitney Block, Title Section, Sixth Floor, Room 6645, Queen's Park, Toronto, Ontario, M7A 1W3.

The districts of the north were divided into townships, most of which land has remained undeveloped and is still owned by the Crown.

Few changes were made in the internal territorial division of the province until 1953, when the Regional Municipality of Toronto was established. Since then, new regional and district municipalities have been created. Counties have been reconstructed, new municipal corporations have been created, municipalities have been amalgamated, area municipalities have been constituted and many municipalities have been affected by annexation.

Part I

THE REGISTRY ACT

CHAPTER 2

THE REGISTRY ACT

The Registry system is governed by the Registry Act, R.S.O. 1980, c. 445, originally enacted by the Legislature of Ontario in 1795. It provided that all dealings with land be registered so the public would have notice of all transactions. Unregistered interests have no effect against registered ones. Land Registrars are appointed to administer the offices.

Amendments to the Land Titles Act, R.S.O. 1980, c. 230, to provide a merging of the Registry and Land Titles systems have been legislated. To accommodate the merging the Land Registration Reform Act, 1984, S.O. 1984, c. 32, provided new document forms and computer indexed files which will eventually replace the manual operation of both systems.

The two systems differ in that the Registry system has been a register for documents and the Land Titles system a register for titles.

Under the Registry Act a 40 year search of title was required, *i.e.,* evidence of title for 40 years prior to the date of the deed to the present registered owner, plus whatever time was necessary prior to the 40 year period to establish a root of title. Recent legislation changed this period and it is explained in Chapter 3 under "The Root".

PATENT

Our first settlers acquired title to land by the grant of a Crown Patent issued by the province pursuant to the provisions of the Public Lands Act, R.S.O. 1980, c. 413. A Crown Patent is a document in which title to land, subject to certain reservations, is passed from the Crown to the patentee, his heirs and assigns. Notice of the granting of the Patent is forwarded to the Land Registrar of the appropriate Registry or Land Titles Office, who records the date, patentee's name and a brief description of the land in an index referred to as an abstract book. If more than one lot is granted, a page is opened for each lot and subsequent registrations are recorded thereon. Crown land is owned by the province and patented lands by registered owner. Subsequent grants of land are usually by conveyance.

Unfortunately, Patents are not on file in either of these offices, except in the case of those issued subsequent to October 1, 1965. Prior to that date, the original Patent was given to the patentee who frequently neglected to register it. Copies of original Patents may be purchased at the Ministry of Government Services, Official Document Section, Third Floor, Hearst Block, Queen's Park, Toronto, that is, if you have the owners' name. If not, copies may be obtained at the Ministry of Natural Resources, Whitney Block, Title Section, Sixth Floor, Room 6645, Queen's Park, Toronto, where there is an index of all Crown land in Ontario. Because of the rugged character of most of the land in the province, 87 per cent of it is still owned by the Crown. The greater part of it has been mapped and that is the only record we have of it.

There are also Crown Patents granted for lands which were originally vested in the Crown in the right of Canada for Indian reservations. They are filed at the Federal Indian Lands Registry. Certified copies are obtainable, free, by writing to: Hubert Ryan, Registrar, Indian Lands Registry, Department of Indian Affairs and Northern Development, Terrasses de la Chaudière, 10 Wellington Street, Hull, Quebec, K1A 0H4.

Unless the Crown Patent grants the bed of navigable water or streams bordering or passing through a parcel of land, title to the bed or streams does not pass. Patents often contain reservations for minerals, pine trees and road allowances so they should be carefully reviewed, particularly for cottage properties and lands outside urban areas such as Toronto.

TITLE BY PRESCRIPTION

Where land is registered under the Registry system, title may also be acquired by adverse possession under the Limitations Act, R.S.O. 1980, c. 240, except in the case of road allowances or highways where the freehold is vested in the Crown or in the municipality. Section 3(1) of the Act also provides that Her Majesty must bring such action for recovery within 60 years or she is barred.

If the occupant of the land can produce evidence by way of a declaration that he has been in possession and occupation of the land for ten years or more prior to the date of closing the transaction, that his possession has been undisturbed throughout by any claim and that he has made no acknowledgment in writing to any person of that person's right to the land, then he can claim possessory title to the land. The declaration should be deposited on title. Title is acquired by a negative right rather than a positive. The registered owner loses his right to object to the trespasser's occupation after an appropriate time.

Similarly, where a right of way or other easement has been enjoyed by a trespasser for 20 years or more without interruption, and without the owner's consent or permission, or without agreement in writing, the trespasser acquires title by possession or prescription. Adverse possession is unique to the Registry system. It is not possible under the Land Titles system.

TITLE BY ACCRETION

Water lines have changed considerably since the original surveys were drawn. You may find that the 66 foot road allowance along the shoreline of a lake reserved in the Crown Patent is now under water.

Where land is extended beyond the shore by gradual and imperceptible retirement of water, the land so extended belongs to the owner of the land. If the extension is sudden and perceptible, it vests in the Crown. Alternatively, where water gradually encroaches on land, such land belongs to the owner of the shore between the low and high water marks. The marks are established by a surveyor.

TITLE BY TAX SALE

When the Municipal Tax Sales Act, 1984, S.O. 1984, c. 48 was legislated, the tax sale provisions in the Municipal Act and the Municipal Affairs Act were repealed. If tax arrears are owing, the treasurer of the municipality may register a tax arrears certificate against the title to the land. Section 4(1) provides that within 60 days thereof, a notice of the registration should be sent to the following persons:

1. the assessed owner of the land;
2. the assessed tenant in occupation of the land;
3. persons named on the abstract book or land titles register or the execution index as having an interest in the land.

The spouse of the person recorded in the land registration office as the owner or the assessed tenant should also be notified, s. 4(2).

A statutory declaration regarding notices is registered in the appropriate land registration office.

A tax arrears certificate may be cancelled by paying the cancellation price to the municipality within one year and registering a certificate of cancellation on title.

One year after the date of registration of a tax arrears certificate the land shall be offered for public sale or auction. If a sale does not occur, it vests in the municipality.

If a sale does take place under s. 5(5), a tax deed or notice of vesting if it goes to the municipality should be registered on title and an estate in fee simple vests in the person named thereon, or in the municipality subject to the following:

1. easements or restrictions that run with the land;
2. any estate or interest of the Crown in the right of Canada or Ontario;
3. an interest or title acquired by adverse possession by abutting owners before registration of the tax deed or the notice of vesting.

On registration of the tax deed a new root of title is created, and a prior search thereto need include only the provisions the land is subject to.

ABSTRACT BOOKS

Under the Registry system all registrations subsequent to the Crown Patent are recorded in an abstract book in the order of their registration. The abstract books contain a brief reference to every registered document commencing with the Crown Patent. The originals of the documents, except the patent, are filed in the Registry Office and may be examined upon request.

Prior to the subdivision of lands, the abstract books are referred to as concession books and after subdivision as plan books. Searching in the concession book is commonly referred to as "going behind the plan". Concession books usually comprise more than one volume especially in offices where the old books have not been re-copied. At the top of each page the concession and lot numbers are recorded for your convenience.

A new abstract book is opened on registration of the following:

1. a plan of subdivision;
2. new municipalities as they are incorporated, and
3. patented lands (concession lots).

The land registrar makes a brief entry of the registration number and date, the owner and the chargee/mortgagee, first in the book of origin, that is, the lot on a concession lot or a prior registered plan currently re-subdivided.

Anyone will direct you to the counter where the abstract books are filed. Upon receipt of a written request (the form is provided by the Registry Office) showing the lot and plan or concession and lot number and the municipality, and on paying the prescribed fee, one may have the use of the books. Most offices display signs to aid you in finding the various departments of the Registry Office.

Sample pages from an abstract book are illustrated on pages 13 to 15. The search outlined in this book was prepared therefrom.

LOT 1   CONCESSION 2   WEST OF YONGE ST.   TWP. OF YORK

NO.	INSTRUMENT	DATE	REG'N. DATE	GRANTOR	GRANTEE	CONSID'TION	DESCRIPTION
	PATENT		1 Nov. 1860	The Crown	Jos. Gray		All - 200 Ac.
234	MTG	3 Oct. 1895	31 Dec. 1895	Joseph Gray	Peter Kelso		W¼ of N½ Ac- 50 Ac.
969	DEED	4 Jul. 1898	5 Oct. 1901	Joseph Gray	John J. Long		PT.20 Ac-RESER'G A R.O.W.
1020	DISCH. MTG	3 Aug. 1901	1 Nov. 1901	Peter Kelso	Jos. Gray		MTG. 234
TWP. NORTH YORK incorporated - 18 July 1922							
724	GRANT	3 Jan. 22	7 Feb. 22	Joseph Gray	Eldon Jones	$1.	Pt. com'g 150'S. from N.W.<; TH SLY 510'±; TH ELY 1650'; TH N.WLY 1560'± to P.O.C. Subj. to restrictions.
1198	MTG	5 Jun. 48	9 Jul. 48	Joseph Gray	Royal Bank		Land in 234
PLAN 4340		7 Oct. 50	1 Dec. 50	Joseph Gray - owner Royal Bank - mtgee			Land in 234
102	DEPOSIT						Part
1945	EXOR.	2 Jun. 53	5 Aug. 1953	Joseph Acton	Peter Garnet	$1.	Part inal - com'g. 70'W. from the N.E.<; TH N74°W 100'; TH S 16°W 100'; TH N 74° E 25'; TH S 17°E 10'; TH N 74°20'10"E 125'; TH N 16°W 100' to P.O.C.
345GR	CONSENT	3 Jul. 53	5 Aug. 53	Treasurer of Ont.	Este. of Jos. Gray		Part

LOT 4   PLAN 4340   TWP. OF NORTH YORK

NO.	INSTRUM'T	DATED	DATE	GRANTOR	GRANTEE	CON.	
PLAN	4340	7 Oct. 50	1 Dec. 50	Joseph Gray - owner			All INAL
1200	BY-LAW	1 Jan. 54	7 Jan. 54	THE CORP'N OF THE TWP. OF NORTH YORK	CREATING AN AREA OF SUBDIVISION CONTROL AND DEEMING LAND IN PLAN 4340 NOT TO BE WITHIN A REG'D. PLAN OF SUBDIVISION		ALL INAL subj. to a MTG.
1215	GRANT	4 Jan. 54	5 Jul. 54	Joseph Gray	John Paul	$1	
1821	DISCHGE	1 Jul. 58	9 Jul. 58	Royal Bank	J. Long, Exec'or of Jos. Gray		MTG. 1198
2231	MTG	5 Jul. 58	9 Jul. 58	John Paul	Joy Builders Ltd.	30,000.	ALL INAL
2304	M.L.	8 Dec. 58	8 Dec. 58	Star Lumber Co.	John Paul	6,000.	ALL INAL
2799	CERT. OF ACTION ON M.L.	7 Jan. 59	9 Jan. 59	Supreme Court of Ontario	John Paul		M.L. #2304
3999	Grant under P. of S.	1 Aug. 1960	3 Aug. 60	John Paul	Joy Builders Ltd.	$1.	ALL INAL
PLAN	6183	3 Jul. 60	4 Dec. 60	Joy Builders Ltd.			ALL INAL

LOT 22   PLAN 6183   TWP. OF NORTH YORK

NO.	INSTRUM'T.	DATE	DATE REG'N.	GRANTOR	GRANTEE	CONSID'TION	DESCRIPTION
PLAN	6183	3 Jul. 60	4 Nov. 60	Joy Builders Ltd.			ALL INAL
8444	AGRT.	1 Nov. 60	6 Dec. 60	Joy Builders Ltd.	The Corp'n of Twp. of North York		ALL INAL
9302	MTG	1 Nov. 60	7 Dec. 60	Joy Builders Ltd.	Eldon Troy	$25,000.00	ALL
17342	GRANT	7 Oct. 60	10 Dec. 60	Joy Builders Ltd.	John J. Jones	$1.	ALL - subj. to MTG over rear 4'
28944	GRANT of Easm't	2 Jan. 61	7 Jan. 61	John J. Jones	Bell Telephone Co. of Canada		
82567	GRANT	8 Aug. 65	6 Sep. 65	John J. Jones	John Santos	$1.	W$1/2$ - subj. to easement MTG 9302
103999	DISCHARGE	15 Jun. 66	15 Jun. 66	Eldon Troy	Joy Builders Ltd.		

BOROUGH OF NORTH YORK - INCORPORATED JAN. 1, 1967

NO.	INSTRUM'T.	DATE	DATE REG'N.	GRANTOR	GRANTEE	CONSID'TION	DESCRIPTION
64R2342	REFERENCE PLAN	6 Jul. 78					PARTS 1 AND 2
1938768	GRANT	1 Jul. 78	10 Jul. 78	John Santos	Winston Croy	$1.	PART 1 on R-PLAN 64R-3242 Subject to an easm't over PART 2

CITY OF NORTH YORK - INCORPORATED FEB. 14, 1979

CHAPTER 3

THE FORTY YEAR SEARCH

Under the Registry system, a solicitor arranges for a forty year search of title to be carried out for the lands the vendor claims to own. The agreement of purchase and sale provides the lot and plan number, the owner's name, and particulars of charges/mortgages to be assumed and those to be discharged. He passes on this information to the title searcher, along with a survey, if one is available.

The responsibility for establishing the ownership of land and whether or not the owner has a good and marketable title lies with the title searcher. The search is the basis for the lawyer's title decision and, if all the relevant material is not provided, the lawyer may be liable to his client for professional negligence. A title searcher should have the ability to work without supervision and to be decisive under demanding circumstances.

The following steps are necessary to complete a search and detailed instructions are provided in subsequent paragraphs:

1. establish a chain of title prior to the registered owner, for forty years or more, by name;
2. establish a root;
3. establish a chain of title subsequent to the root, by description;
4. prepare an abstract of title;
5. requisition and read the documents;
6. search abutting lands where applicable;
7. prepare graphic outlines of the relevant lands, and adjoining lands where they are not indicated on surveys or plans;
8. search executions;
9. prepare a summary.

Presume that you have been requested to complete a forty year search of the east half of lot 22, Plan 6183 in the Borough of North York, and that the registered owner is John Jones. See diagram on page 20.

Normally, one determines which system land is registered under from the plan of subdivision. When the letter "M", or the Land Titles

Office number and the letter M, *e.g.*, "66M", or the letter "D" or "Misc", prefixes the plan number, the land is under the Land Titles system.

Plan 6183 was registered under the Registry system. Plans of subdivision under that system are numbered consecutively, followed by the municipality, *i.e.*, Plan 6183, Borough of North York.

In the case of land that has not been subdivided, it is described by lot and concession number, *i.e.*, lot 3, concession VI, Township of North York.

If you do not have the necessary reference to obtain the abstract book, municipal maps illustrating concession lots and others indicating plans of subdivision are provided by the Registry Office for your convenience. Failing that, a search of the local municipal assessment office indexes will provide it.

The plan book and the white print of Plan 6183 (a white print is a copy of the original), are your first requirements in commencing a search. You may wish to make a sketch from the original plan — a time consuming effort and usually only attempted when white prints are not available. The white print will provide you with the following information:

1. the boundaries of the plan in solid line;
2. the date of registration of the plan;
3. the registered owner;
4. the surveyor, survey monuments and astronomic north;
5. the lands subdivided, *e.g.*, a plan of subdivision of lot 4, Plan 4340, Township of North York;
6. the dimensions and bearings of the lot to be searched, and the adjoining lots, blocks and reserves;
7. easements;
8. roads and their widenings and closings, and one foot reservations and their dedications;
9. the relation of lot 22 on Plan 6183 to lot 4 on Plan 4340, *i.e.*, lot 22 is situated in the south east corner of lot 4 and commences 120 feet south from its north west angle and runs southerly 60 feet by 45 feet easterly;
10. approval of the Planning Act.

Presume that the subject land was subdivided by Plan 6183 in 1960, only 20 years ago. You will obviously have to search prior to 1960 for a root of title. The white print indicates that Plan 6183 is a re-subdivision of lots 4 and 5 on Plan 4340 of the Township of North York (Boroughs were established January 1, 1967).

Your next requirement is the abstract book and white print for Plan 4340 (new forms and fees for subsequent books are not required). The white print indicates that Plan 4340 was registered in 1950, 30 years ago, and that it is a subdivision of lot 1, concession II, west of Yonge Street. So now, refer to the concession book for lot 1, concession II. Fortunately, its entries go back to the Crown Patent so there are no more books to examine.

Once a plan has been registered an entry is made in the concession and plan abstract books of particulars of registration, the registered owner and prior mortgagees. At this point, dispense with the concession book because all the entries for the lands, now subdivided, are entered in the plan book, except for deposits. Since they provide evidence of some fact relating to prior title the description will be that of the prior title.

The white print of the plan of subdivision in this case indicates that the north west angle of lot 4, Plan 4340 commences 150 feet south from the north west angle of lot 1, concession 2 and runs southerly 180 feet by 150 feet easterly. The diagram on page 20 clarifies the relation of the plan to the concession lot. On referring to the concession book, in the description column you will find reference to all of the north west quarter of lot 1. Obviously, Plan 4340 will be contained in that description.

I must add that it is unusual for a plan to be re-subdivided as in this case. Better still, you don't always have to refer to the concession book because many plans have been registered for 40 years and more. However, there are lands that have not been subdivided and in that case the concession book only is required — the entries for all 200 acres, or whatever acreage the lot contains must be examined.

THE ROOT

The commencing point of a search is referred to as the root and a good root of title is a conveyance most recently registered before the 40 year period. The following are not considered good roots:

1. a grant under power of sale in a mortgage — it depends on the terms of the mortgage;
2. a quit claim deed, which is a release of someone else's interest.

The following, although not registered for 40 years, are considered to be good roots. It is advisable to check with one's solicitor prior to using 2, 3 or 4 as a root.

1. A Patent from the Crown. The land may be subject to reservations so many solicitors wish to review the document.
2. A conveyance from the Director, The Veterans' Land Act. After World War II, the Director, The Veterans' Land Act purchased lands for resale to veterans. Such grants had the same effect as a Crown grant and are generally considered to be a good root of title.

Subdivision and Re-subdivision of Part of a Concession Lot

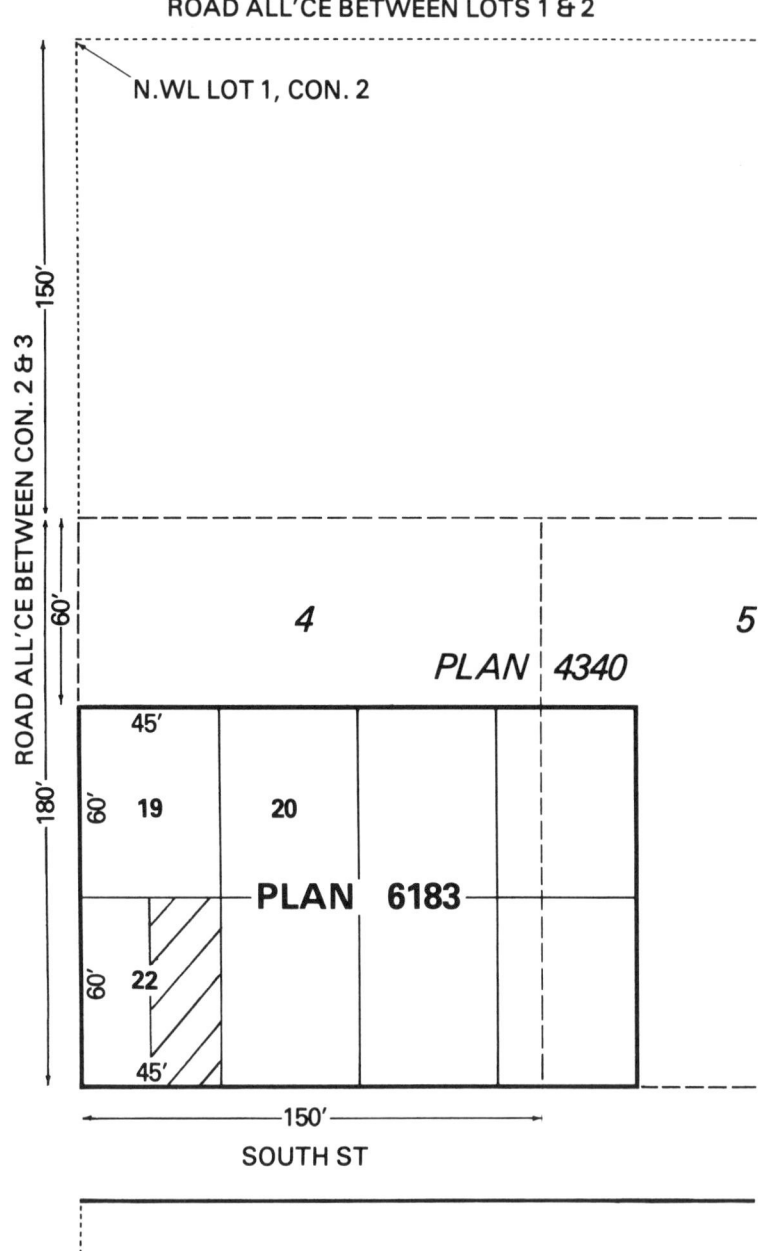

Diagram Illustrating a Concession Lot Parcel

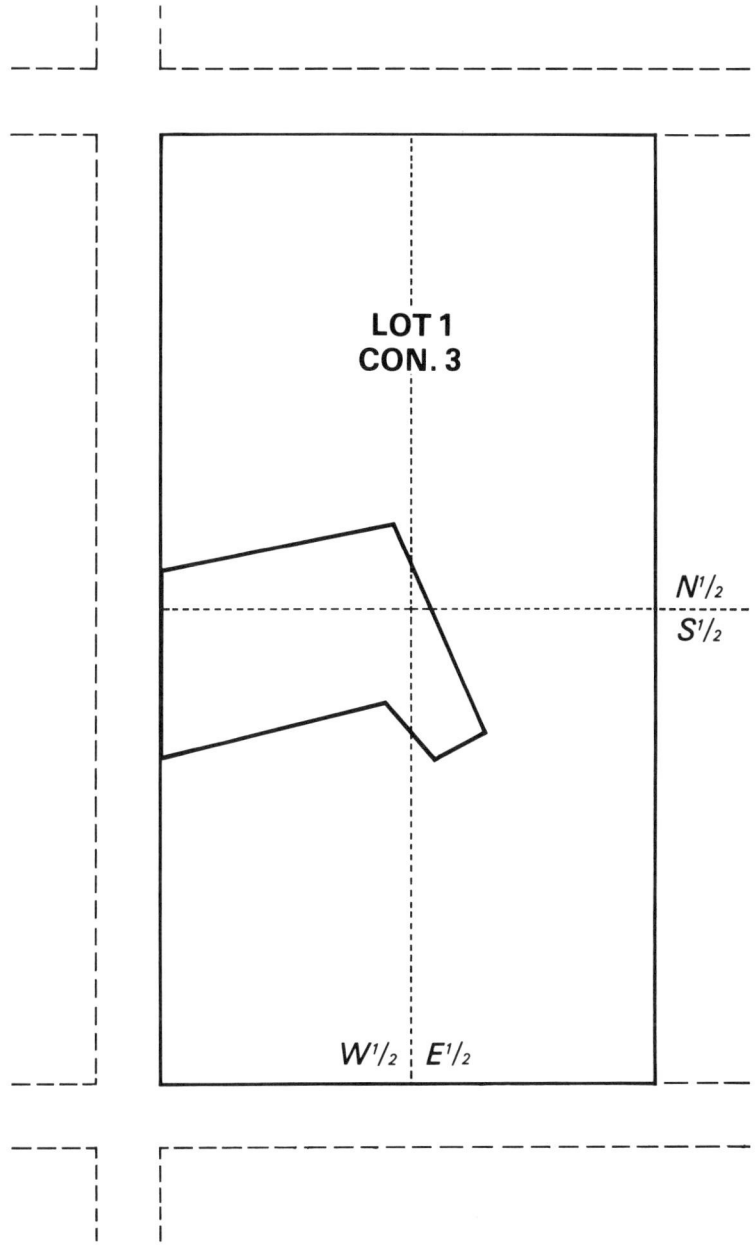

LOT 1
CON. 3

$N^1/_2$
$S^1/_2$

$W^1/_2$ $E^1/_2$

3. A tax deed.
4. Pursuant to the Expropriations Act, R.S.O. 1980, c. 148, s. 9(1), where a proposed expropriation has been approved under this Act, or under the Ontario Energy Board Act, R.S.O. 1980, c. 332, the land vests in the expropriating authority on registration of a plan of the lands in the appropriate Registry Office. The plan must be signed by the expropriating authority and an Ontario Land Surveyor.
5. An executor's or administrator's deed, since the Registry Amendment Act, S.O. 1981, c. 17.

The above points 2, 3 and 4 are always subject to restrictive covenants, and easements registered on prior title. It is the duty of the searcher to provide evidence as to whether or not they exist.

The Registry Amendment Act, S.O. 1981, c. 17, which came into force on August 1, 1981, provides for reduction of the search period to 40 years. The necessity for establishing a good root prior to that period was eliminated, except as provided in the amendment. The amendment of Part III generated many inquiries. The interpretation of the legislation, by the legal staff of the Property Rights Division, Land Registration Improvement Project, Ministry of Consumer and Commercial Relations, is that the title search period is limited to and does not exceed 40 years. A chain of title does not depend upon and is not affected by any document registered before the commencement of the title search period except:

(a) Where there has been no conveyance (other than a mortgage) within the title search period, the chain of title commences with the first conveyance before the 40 year period.
(b) Where a document is protected by a notice registered within the title search period. Section 112(2) retains the notice procedure. A new form will be prescribed by regulation. It should be noted that a claim older than 40 years is no longer preserved by reference to it in a document registered within the search period (e.g., a will).
(c) Where there is a claim referred to in s. 112(5), which generally carries forward the exceptions in the previous s. 112(2).

Further clarification provided that, where there is no conveyance within the title search period, the chain of title begins with the first conveyance prior to commencement of the 40 year period, s. 111(2). Any interest set out in that root deed still affects the land (a right-of-way or easement, for example). However, it is the opinion of many solicitors that documents registered between that root deed and the beginning of the title search period have expired, unless a notice is registered to preserve them, s. 111(3). It is their view that they can be eliminated from the search.

Other solicitors feel that they would be negligent if they failed to establish a chain of title which commenced prior to the new 40 year title search period and which extended through that period. On this important subject, title searchers should consult their solicitors.

A 25 year search of title period is still under review by the Land Registration Improvement Project.

CHAIN OF TITLE BY NAME

The next step is to set up a chain of title by tracing the registered owners on prior title for 40 years, or as long as it takes to set up a good root of title. This is usually a fairly straightforward exercise; from the registered owner John Jones follow the grants to the prior owners until a root of title is established. A proper investigation of the books requires attention to detail to avoid missing a document.

Occasionally, missing links occur and it is necessary to attempt to establish the root first. Where the next-of-kin of an intestate in whom the land vested after three years conveys, you will not find a grant to that person in the chain of title. A search in the General Register index under the name of the previous registered owner will reveal if administration had been granted, or if a declaration declaring the facts of the death of the intestate had been deposited on title.

A change of name resulting from marriage or divorce can slow the pace when tracing names. The next deed on title or a deposit usually contains recitals or a declaration that clarifies the situation.

In the past century people were not too concerned about registering deeds. You may find a deed registered 20 July, 1969 which was dated 3 August, 1865, so it is often practical to check recent registrations when a link is missing.

When the entries indicate that Jas. Craig owns four different parcels, the description may show that the subject land is contained in one or maybe two of the parcels, or even that it is a part of all four, as the diagram on page 21 illustrates. Prior title may reveal that he purchased all four parts in four deeds from four different parties. That problem is clarified in the chain illustrated on page 24, and you will be glad to know that it is not a common one. I emphasize it here to impress upon you the importance of finding all the parts — the missing part may be subject to an easement or a mortgage, etc.

CHAIN OF TITLE BY DESCRIPTION

After a chain has been established by name, the next step is to check the description in all subsequent entries and to list all the numbers that

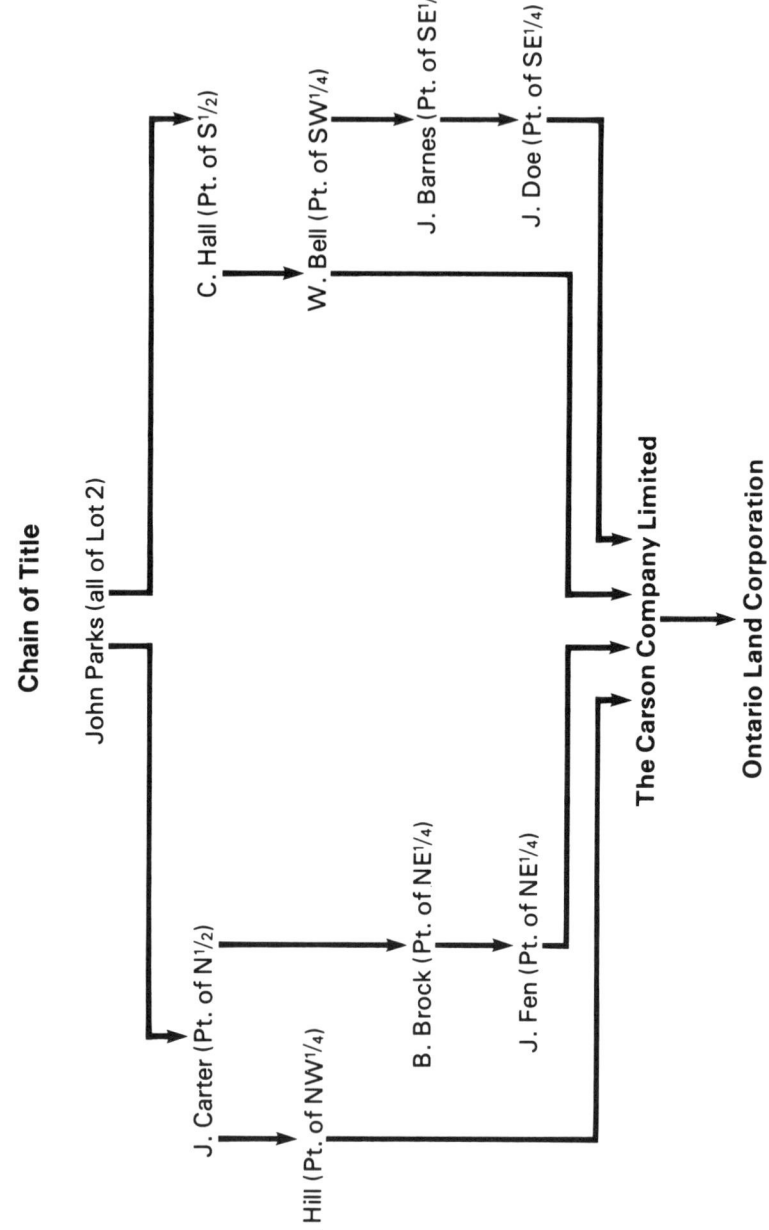

affect the subject lands. The abstract books contain only a condensed description of the land.

Often, particularly in small registry offices, the description in the abstract book reads "part," meaning a part of the lot. To determine which part, it is necessary to requisition the documents and examine the description therein. It may be frustrating but there is no other way of establishing whether or not the documents affect the subject lands. "Part inal," means part of the lands described in the document and other lands.

As parts of the original lands are sold off, less land is usually granted in subsequent deeds, *e.g.*, the grantor owned the north half of the concession lot and sold only the west half of the north half, retaining the east half of the north half.

Descriptions for lands that have been severed, particularly a parcel severed from a concession lot, are often difficult to plot, but the sections on land descriptions and metes and bounds descriptions should help to resolve any problems that arise.

ABSTRACT OF TITLE

After a chain of title has been established, the particulars recorded in the abstract book of the relevant entries should be recorded on your search paper (commonly referred to as an abstract paper) in chronological order. Space is required for document contents and and solicitor's remarks, so for practical purposes record one entry to each page.

The abstract is a recording of the following documents: grants or deeds; grants under power of sale; final orders of foreclosure; mortgages and their assignments and discharges; mortgages of mortgages; leases and their releases; deposits; notices of conditional sales; construction liens, their certificates of action and discharges; *Lis Pendens*; cautions; tax arrears certificates; tax deeds; by-laws; agreements; certificates; consents; notices of security interest and annexation orders.

On completion you have what is known as an abstract of title. Note the registration number only of the last document recorded in the abstract book, whether or not it affects the subject lands, and the date of completion of the search to indicate where a subsearch should commence, and number the pages consecutively.

Needless to say, a title searcher's handwriting and manner of layout should be clearly expressed. This is often overlooked when it is necessary to expedite a search the same day, but it will make the solicitor happy when preparing the letter of requisitions.

REQUISITION AND READ DOCUMENTS

Now, requisition the documents on the forms provided by the Registry Office. Completion of the forms in detail may save you much time later. The reference G.R. or DEPOSIT should be noted on the form, where applicable. There is a fee for each one ordered. While you wait for them to be located you may find it worth your while to re-check the abstract book — it is easy to miss an entry. If you are ever in doubt as to whether or not a document affects the subject land, record it — let the solicitor decide its validity. You will never be reprimanded for writing too much. All the documents should be read, and in chronological order.

Refer to the chapter on documents and affidavits — also the sections on surveys and descriptions — for the particulars to be recorded on your search.

LAND DESCRIPTIONS

Land descriptions incorporated in a document are probably the most interesting feature of searching titles but often pose a special challenge. However, since the advent of reference plans in 1973, there are considerably fewer problems to deal with.

On commencing a search, if a survey is not available, or if a plan or a sketch is not attached to a document, time may be saved by preparing a sketch from the description in the first deed and noting errors and omissions in subsequent descriptions.

Plans found on title are not always full plans of survey and do not contain sufficient information for a solicitor to form a title opinion. The legal description in the deed, especially old deeds, does not always correspond with the boundary the surveyor established. Notes should be made of any irregularities in dimensions and bearings.

When placing new monumentation the surveyor must attempt to re-establish the original boundary, not the limit described in the deed.

Original boundaries are proven by evidence of natural boundaries (lakes, *etc.*), or by proof of the location of the original undisturbed monumentation or other evidence as to where they were located, and, as a last resort, by the limits as described in the deed.

The description in subsequent deeds must be checked verbatim with the first and against the plans or sketches to ensure that exactly the same land is granted each time. To determine if there are any encroachments on your land check the abutting lands descriptions against the description for the subject lands. The boundaries must coincide exactly.

For the sake of accuracy and time, obtain copies of long complicated descriptions and particularly of those in error. The descriptions in old documents and on old plans are usually in chains and links. Although the occasion to use them does not arise often, a chart to facilitate conversion has been included in Appendix 1.

THE SURVEY

A plan of survey is certified by a land surveyor who attends at the site and defines the boundaries of a parcel of land. He is usually requested to site thereon buildings, rights-of-way, easements, lanes, roads, fences, water courses, trees, elevations, monumentation and measurements. The description in the registered documents should conform with the survey. Also, record its date and any building encroachments.

In addition, if building restrictions have been registered, the set back and coverage requirements should be checked with the survey.

THE SKETCH

A sketch is prepared by someone other than a surveyor, for the purpose of illustrating a description. They are often attached to old documents to illustrate a complex description and are usually sketches prepared by a title searcher.

METES AND BOUNDS DESCRIPTIONS

Undeveloped lands are usually described in an uncomplicated manner, *i.e.*:

1. the whole of the lot;
2. the south half of the lot;
3. the south half of the north half of the lot, *etc.*

Where land boundaries are parallel to the original lot line the description is easy to follow. A parcel having a frontage of 100 feet on the road allowance by 400 feet deep and running westerly from the north east corner would be described as follows:

commencing at the north east corner of lot 2;
thence southerly along the east limit of the said lot, 100 feet to a point;
thence westerly and parallel to the north limit of the said lot, 400 feet to a point;
thence northerly and parallel to the east limit of the said lot, 100 feet more or less to a point in the north limit of the said lot;
thence easterly along the north limit of the said lot, 400 feet more or less to the point of commencement.

The term "more or less" is a protection against minor discrepancies in legal descriptions; the measure is not as important as the fact that the line must reach the east limit, or the point of commencement, whichever it may be — there cannot be a gap.

In the case of a parcel of land where the boundaries are not parallel, a surveyor is engaged to prepare a metes and bounds description. The description can be a challenge, but title searchers usually become quite skilled at interpretation, and at detecting changes or errors from one document to another.

The surveyor uses bearings to define the relationship of a line to north and south and they are similar to compass directions which are given as:

1. east or west of north
   e.g., north 74 degrees west on a description means a line which is 74 degrees west of north;
2. east or west of south
   e.g., south 18 degrees 16 minutes east means a line which is 18 degrees 16 minutes east of south.

The most common unit for measuring angles is the degree, which is defined as 1/360 of a circle.

Diagram to Illustrate Bearings

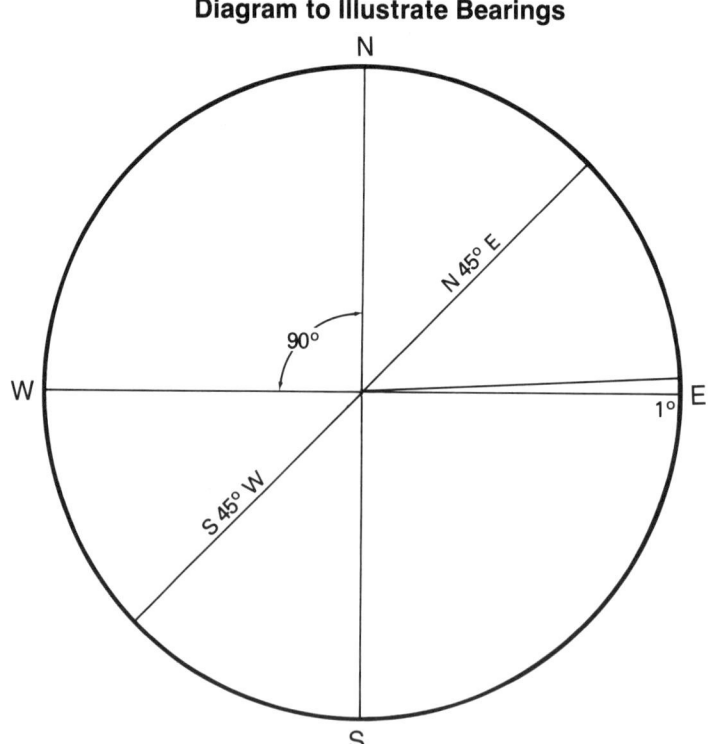

A circle contains 360 degrees°
A degree contains 60 minutes'
A minute contains 60 seconds"

Every line has two directions: note diagram on page 28. The diagonal line proceeding towards the top of the page has a bearing of 45 degrees east of north, written as north 45 degrees east. When the line proceeds in the opposite direction it has a bearing of 45 degrees west of south, written as south 45 degrees west.

Curved lines are often difficult to follow. The arc length, radius and chord length and chord bearing are a part of the description. Note that a curve to the right will curve in a clockwise direction and a curve to the left will curve in a counter-clockwise direction. The arc of a curve to the right will always be to the left of a chord, when facing in the direction of the chord and vice versa.

The following description and the diagram on page 30 illustrate bearings in a metes and bounds description.

In the City of Brantford, in the County of Brant and being composed of part of Lot 61 according to Plan 141, registered in the Registry Office for the Registry Division of Brant.

Premising that all bearings herein are referred to the western limit of Woodlawn Avenue, in the City of Brantford, being north 13°44'55" west.

Commencing at the north east corner of Lot 61, registered Plan 141; thence south easterly on a curve to the right, having a radius of 150.00 feet, an arc distance of 20.23 feet (the chord equivalent being 20.23 feet measured north 17°36'45" west) to a point in the east limit of said Lot 61;

thence south 13°44'55" east along the eastern limit of said Lot 61, a distance of 38.76 feet more or less to the south east corner of said Lot 61;

thence south 76°15'05" west along the southern limit of said Lot 61, a distance of 60.75 feet more or less to a point in the said southern limit;

thence north 23°52'05" west, to a point in the north limit of said Lot 61, a distance of 30.00 feet more or less;

thence north 62°58'50" east along the northern limit of said Lot 61, a distance of 80.13 feet to the north east corner and the point of commencement.

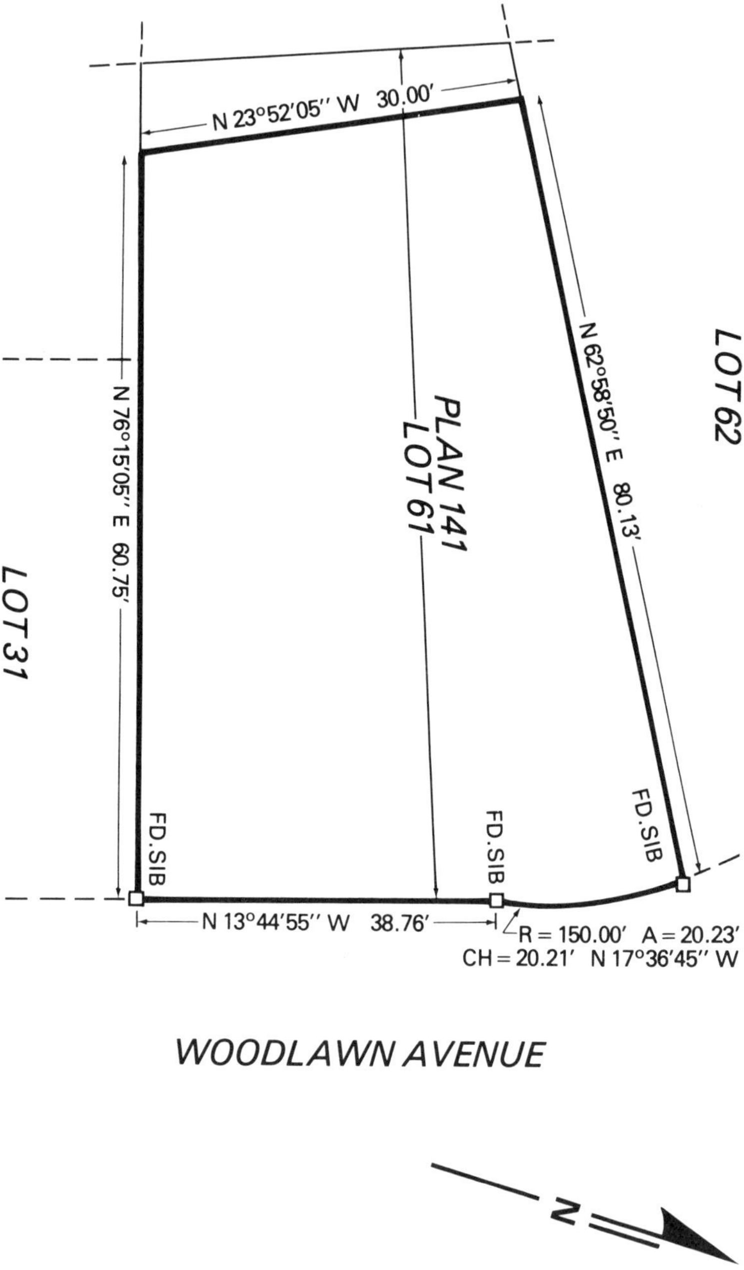

N 23°52'05" W 30.00'

N 76°15'05" E 60.75'

N 62°58'50" E 80.13'

PLAN 141
LOT 61

LOT 62

LOT 31

FD. SIB

FD. SIB

FD. SIB

N 13°44'55" W 38.76'

R = 150.00' A = 20.23'
CH = 20.21' N 17°36'45" W

WOODLAWN AVENUE

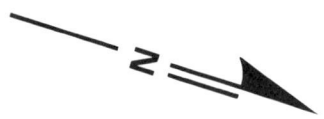

NEW MUNICIPAL BOUNDARIES

Where new municipal boundaries have been established by dividing existing municipalities among two or more municipalities, an entry is made on the abstract book or parcel register.

If the land being searched is in the "Counties of Lincoln and Welland" and they have been renamed "Regional Municipality of Niagara", you will find "Regional Municipality of Niagara" noted on the book or register.

Following that, the description in subsequent registered documents should contain the prior designation and "now in the Regional Municipality of Niagara" or, where there are no further registrations, record the amendment on your search notes.

REGULATIONS

Ontario Regulation 898, R.R.O. 1980, provides certain requirements for descriptions in documents tendered for registration in a land registration office.

Where the deed/transfer to the vendor does not conform with the following requirements, title search notes should indicate that the description is unacceptable for use in subsequent documents:

1. Lots must be enumerated, 1, 2, 3 and 4, not lots 1 to 4, s. 54(1)(a).
2. Where the bearings of lines are in degrees, the origin of the bearings should be stated in the description (description page 29 and survey page 30); they relate to the bearing of the road allowance, s. 54(1)(c)(i).
3. Descriptions for curved boundaries shall include the arc lengths, the radius, the chord length and chord bearing, s. 54(1)(c)(ii).
4. The description for part of a lot shall refer to at least one of the corners of the lot, and shall give the distance from that corner to an angle of the part being described, s. 51(1)(c)(iii).
5. Symbols may be used in place of the words, degrees, minutes and seconds, but not for feet and inches, s. 54(1)(c)(iv).
6. Capital letters, N S E and W, may be substituted for north, south, east and west with respect to bearings in degrees. Other words may not be abbreviated or contracted, s. 54(1)(c)(iv).
7. Land shall not be described by exception, s. 51(1)(d), *i.e.,* "all lot 10, concession IV, except that part previously granted by document number 45789". A reference plan must now be prepared for the exception, except in the following cases:
   (a) a description repeated in a document prior to July 1, 1964;
   (b) the whole of the land on a registered plan of subdivision;
   (c) a railway line, or right-of-way of a railway company, or a public

street, road or highway laid out on an original survey or shown on a registered plan;

  (d) a parcel completely surrounded by the land described in the document, or

  (e) a designated PART on a reference plan or plan of expropriation.

8. A boundary line may not be described by reference to a registered document number, *i.e.*, "thence northerly to the south limit of land described in document registered number 16789". However, a document number may be used, provided measurements and other compliances are observed, s. 54(1)(e).

9. Imperial units or metric units shall be used, s. 54(1)(f). Subdivision of the units requires decimals to describe fractions, except that inches are still acceptable where the description is the same as in a previous document, s. 54(4).

10. The new and former designation provided for reorganized municipal boundaries shall be included in all future descriptions prepared for documents, *i.e.*, "in the Town of Halton Hills, in the Regional Municipality of Halton (formerly the Town of Acton in the County of Halton)", *etc.*, s. 54(1)(b)(ii) and (iii).

11. Land may be described as the south east ¼ of lot 14, concession II, if it was so described in the Crown Patent, and no adjoining part of the said lot is owned by the person dealing with such part, s. 55(d).

12. A parcel of land may still be described as the north half of lot 47 according to registered Plan number 2000, if it was previously so described in a registered document, s. 55(c).

13. The description for part of a street or highway that has been stopped up or closed shall refer to the registration number of the by-law or other document by which it was stopped up or closed, s. 55(h).

14. Notwithstanding any of the foregoing, an unacceptable description used in a deed/transfer to a person now deceased may be used in the administrator's or executor's deed/transfer; likewise in an assignment of a lease, or charge/mortgage an unacceptable description may be repeated, s. 56(2).

METRIC

The International System of Units known the world over as SI (from the French *Système international d'unités*) is the modern version of the metric system. It was adopted in Ontario on July 1, 1976, and since that time, Land Registrars have accepted plans of subdivision, surveys and land descriptions in imperial or metric units.

The metre (m) and decimals thereof are used to express distances, except for the occasional use of kilometres (km) on key maps. Conversion involves basic mathematics. Tables have been provided in Appendix 1 to facilitate the process of relating imperial to metric units.

ROAD ALLOWANCES

Frequently, road allowances shown on the original survey have never been opened, and new surveys show that what appeared to be private property is actually a road allowance.

Crown Patents usually contain the following reservation, "reserving a strip of land 66 feet in width along the shore . . . for a road". This clause has often been misinterpreted. Where the original plan of survey of township lots does not show a road allowance along the shore of the lake the land reserved is not a part of the patentee's land, but is unpatented land, and the patentee does not have legal access to the shore.

The Municipal Act, R.S.O. 1980, c. 302, s. 361(1), (2) and (3), provides that abutting owners have the first right to purchase, to the centre line of road allowances. If they do not exercise the right within the time period as set out in a by-law, then the municipality may sell the road allowance to other interested parties. The sale should be under the authorization of a by-law of the particular municipality. This problem is particularly common in cottage country.

Approvals must be obtained for the proper closing of any road allowance and it is important to note on your search the identity of the approving party and registration number of the closing by-law. Also, where part of a highway laid out on a plan of subdivision registered after March 27, 1946 is closed, the by-law is not effective until it has been approved by the Minister of Housing. Occasionally, you may find that part of the land that you have been requested to search forms part of a road allowance, and other lands, *e.g.*, parts of lots 4 and 5, concession 6, and part of the road allowance between the said lots 4 and 5, in the said concession lot. Pages are designated for road allowances in the abstract books, and in small offices an entire book is set aside for all road allowances. A particular sequence was never established and an entry for concession 6 may be followed by an entry for concession 12. The by-laws authorizing opening and closing of road allowances and all other registrations are recorded in the particular abstract books.

PLANS OF SUBDIVISION

The Registry Act, R.S.O. 1980, c. 445, defines a plan of subdivision as a plan by which the owner divides land into designated areas. For the purpose of the Planning Act, it is a plan approved by the Ontario Municipal Board and subsequently registered in the Registry or Land Titles Office.

When a developer decides to construct houses on his land, he must register a plan of subdivision. The name of the person who signs the plan as owner will be recorded on the abstract book as the registered owner. After complying with the Registry and Planning Acts and obtaining approval of the municipality and mortgagees, he lays out lots, blocks, streets and reserves. The bearings of all the boundaries and the dimensions of all the lots, blocks and reserves are shown on the plan. Section 57(1) of the Surveys Act, R.S.O. 1980, c. 493, subject to the Land Titles Act or the Registry Act as to amendments or alteration of plans, provides that every road allowance, highway, street, lane, walk and common shown on a registered plan of subdivision shall be deemed to be a public road, highway, street, lane, walk and common respectively.

Pursuant to s. 73(8) of the Registry Act and s. 150(3) of the Land Titles Act, spousal right of possession under Part III of the Family Law Reform Act, 1978, was released from land dedicated by an owner for a street or public highway.

Now, you have the least complex description (unless a lot has been severed) and it should read, "the whole of lot 5 according to a plan registered in the Registry Office for the Registry Division for Toronto Boroughs as number 2301". Refer now to "Registered Plans", Chapter 9, The Planning Act.

DEEMING BY-LAW — See Chapter 9, The Planning Act

ONE FOOT RESERVE

Subdividers reserve a one foot wide strip of land at the end of streets on the boundaries of the plan of subdivision to prevent anyone from using the streets until the requirements of the subdivision have been completed. Although a reserve has been granted or transferred to the municipality, it is not a public street or highway until it is dedicated as such by a municipal by-law or, alternatively, a notice has been typed on the plan of subdivision to the effect that the one foot reserves thereon are dedicated.

The route from the subject land to a main access highway may be across one or more plans of subdivision. The reserves may be dedicated on the plan being searched but not on the adjoining plans, so the client does not have the right of legal access to a main highway. Evidence of all dedications should be recorded on your search, and you should be aware that to control access along the boundaries of certain lands, usually lands adjacent to busy streets, one foot reserves are created as a permanent arrangement.

The land registrar designates pages at the back of the plan books for the deeds, reserves and by-law entries. It is important that they are examined and particulars noted.

COMPILED PLANS

The purpose of a compiled plan is to clearly identify property boundaries for parcels that were divided over the years by metes and bounds descriptions, and to assist in maintaining proper Registry Office records. They eliminate the aggravation of searching through the volumes containing the entries for an entire concession lot. They are explained in greater detail in Chapter 9, The Planning Act.

PLANS OF EXPROPRIATION

As soon as a plan of expropriation has been registered in the appropriate Registry or Land Titles Office, title vests in the expropriating authority free of all encumbrances, and a deed or transfer is not required to be registered. The plan should be signed by the expropriating authority and an Ontario land surveyor. Consent of the approving authority should be either endorsed on the plan, or reference made to the registration particulars.

REFERENCE PLANS

The introduction of reference plans provided a significant advancement in title searching. The hours spent interpreting old, often inaccurate, descriptions have been greatly reduced. Most important, they eliminate the possibility of error.

The Registry Act, R.S.O. 1980, c. 445, s. 74, requires that after April 1, 1973 a plan of survey certified by an O.L.S. be deposited on title for every severance, unless the land being conveyed or mortgaged is the whole of a lot or block on a registered plan of subdivision, or the whole part remaining to an owner.

Long, complex metes and bounds descriptions are shown graphically, and subsequent descriptions need only be referred to as a "PART". Section 149 of the Land Titles Act, R.S.O. 1980, c. 230, contains a similiar requirement.

They are usually referred to as "R-Plans" and the land on which it is deposited is referred to as a "PART" or "PARTS" on a reference plan. All the PARTS are surveyed and monumented in accordance with the Registry Act.

Each reference plan is allotted a number when it is deposited in the Land Titles or Registry Office and the number is prefixed by the number of such office and the letter "R", *e.g.*, 64R-2341. Originally, they were not prefixed with the number of the Registry or Land Titles Office, only with the letter R, *e.g.*, R-2345.

An appropriate description should read, "That certain parcel . . . composed of parts of lots 11 and 12 according to Plan 6234 which parts are designated PARTS 7 and 8 on a plan of reference filed in the Land Titles Office at Toronto as number 66R-1234."

Section 149 of the Land Titles Act and s. 74(1) of the Registry Act provide that a reference plan is *not* required where:

(a) Pursuant to the Registry Act, the owner conveys or mortgages all the land that he owns as one parcel; and pursuant to the Land Titles Act, the owner conveys or mortgages the whole of the parcel register. The remainder of a parcel is treated as the whole of the parcel.

(b) Pursuant to the Registry Act, the land consists of the whole of a lot, block, street, lane, reserve or common according to a registered plan of subdivision, judge's plan or municipal plan under c. 85; the same applies under the Land Titles Act, except the lot, *etc.*, must be according to a registered plan of subdivision or a composite plan.

(c) The land is the whole of a PART according to a previously deposited reference plan.

Pursuant to s. 149(3) and s. 74(2) the Land Registrar may decide to waive the statutory requirements for a reference plan other than the exceptions in ss. 149 and 74(1). In that event, an order, signed by the Registrar, is stamped on the deed or other document indicating that the description is exempt from the requirement that a reference plan be deposited. A sketch is acceptable under circumstances which are approved by the Land Registrar. A statement, prepared on a schedule, that it is a sketch and not a survey shall be attached to documents presented for registration.

It should be noted that a reference plan is not to be confused with a plan of subdivision under ss. 29, 35 and 36 of the Planning Act, R.S.O. 1980, c. 379. The fact that it is designated a PART on a reference plan in no way changes the position with regard to the Planning Act. Subdivision still applies and part lot control or deeming cannot apply.

RAILWAY ABANDONMENT PLANS

Lands acquired by railway companies were seldom surveyed and the descriptions were so incomplete that they are not acceptable under present day regulations. Many parts of their lands are not used today so the companies are compiling railway property plans of all their lands and preparing new plans showing the lands that they intend to abandon. They are referred to as abandonment plans and are filed as a deposit under Part II of the Registry Act.

They are not reference plans but each parcel is referred to as a "PART" when they are conveyed. A portion of the plan showing the relevant PART should be attached to each deed. Such plans are intended for the initial conveyance from the railway and reference should be made to ss. 74 and 75 of the Registry Act for subsequent conveyances.

BOUNDARIES ACT

Where doubt exists as to the true location of boundary lines, an owner may apply to the Land Registrar under the Boundaries Act, R.S.O. 1980, c. 47, to have a new survey made or the present boundaries confirmed.

Where a new survey is recommended, a certified plan of survey is deposited in the land registration office and it supersedes the prior surveys and description. Of course, adjoining land descriptions should be reviewed carefully: they should conform with the new survey.

RULED IN RED

Documents ruled off in red need not be recorded on your search, provided the ruled line has been initialled and the registration number of the discharge has been noted in the margin. In the past, Land Registrars drew a line through the entries for mortgages and their discharges when the discharge had been registered for ten years or more. Unfortunately, the practice was not kept up and the custom was discontinued in 1972.

Section 51(8) of the Registry Act provided that after a discharge of mortgage had been registered for 10 years or more the land described in the mortgage was not subject to any claim under the mortgage, and the entries for the mortgage, discharge and related documents could be ruled off the abstract index.

Section 51(8) has been amended to require the Land Registrar to rule the entry for the mortgage, discharge and related documents (subs. (6)) immediately after the discharge is registered, as a part of the abstracting procedure, unless, of course, the Land Registrar does not consider the mortgage to be validly discharged. In that event, the discharge will be abstracted as in the past and ruling out will not take place. The title searcher should include it in his abstract of title.

The registration number of the valid discharge will be noted in the margin beside the mortgage and related document entries and signed by an authorized person. It should be noted that the Act continues to provide that where a discharge has been registered for 10 years or more the land is no longer subject to any claim under the mortgage or related documents, even if the entries have not been ruled off (s. 51(11)). The amendments also provide authority to rule off previously discharged mortgages.

Partial discharges and the mortgage may be ruled if a final discharge has been registered and the Land Registrar is satisfied that the Planning Act affidavit, for a consent required since 1973 and affidavit since April 1, 1981, have been complied with in regard to partials.

Section 51(8) of the Registry Act provides that a mortgage, a debenture or a deed of trust and mortgage may be ruled off the abstract book where they have been effectively discharged. The release and re-conveyance of the debenture, deed of trust and mortgage and any supplemental indentures are all ruled off. Documents to which s. 26 of the act applies, *i.e.*, lodgement of title documents and their discharges are also ruled off.

Similarily s. 62(2) provides that where a valid discharge of:

1. a certificate of Lis Pendens
2. a claim for a construction lien
3. a certificate of action in respect to a construction lien
4. a registered notice of a conditional sale contract
5. a registered gas or oil lease

has been registered for two or more years, the land is not affected by any claim and it may be ruled from the abstract page together with its discharge and all other related documents.

ABUTTING LAND SEARCHES

Land may be conveyed without consent under the Planning Act if the owner does not retain the fee or equity of redemption (ownership) in abutting land, s. 49(3)(b) and (5)(a) of the Planning Act, 1983, S.O. 1983, c. 1. Where two parcels abut on a point, they are not considered abutting; they must have a common boundary.

However, there are transactions where lands are not considered to abut and they are listed in Chapter 9. In all other cases, an abstract should be prepared of all abutting owners from June 15, 1967 — the date prior to which contravention of the Act was forgiven.

Of course, you need not search prior to a document registered under the L.R.R.A., 1984, provided the statement that previous conveyances are deemed to comply with s. 49 of the Planning Act, 1983 has been signed by the transferor, transferor's solicitor and transferee's solicitor. If a white print of the plan of subdivision is not available, indicate the abutting lands on the sketch you prepared of the subject lands.

Abutting lands are not always on the same plan of subdivision as the subject lands, or they may even be a part of the concession lot, or they may not be registered in the same land registration office. But these problems are easily resolved.

EXECUTION SEARCH

The final step is the execution search, particulars of which are outlined in Chapter 7.

CERTIFICATION OF TITLE

Certification of title, passed in 1958, eliminates the long 40 year search. It becomes compulsory in certain areas in Ontario for land in proposed plans of subdivision to be investigated and certified.

Pursuant to the Registry Act, R.S.O. 1980, c. 445, s. 73(10) and Ont. Reg. 825/91, the Province of Ontario was designated as a certification area. Accordingly, a plan of subdivision of land registered under the Registry Act will not be accepted for registration under that Act unless a certificate of title has been registered certifying the subdivider to be the owner of the land. This came into force on January 1, 1982.

The Certification of Titles Amendment Act, 1982, S.O. 1982, c. 38, came into force on July 7, 1982. The Director of Titles may now, without application, certify the title to land included in existing plans of subdivision registered under the Registry Act.

The certificate is conclusive evidence that the person named therein as owner has an absolute title to the lands described in the certificate as of the time named therein, subject only to the exceptions and encumbrances shown in the schedules attached thereto. A new root of title has been created, so title searchers need only record the following:

(a) particulars of documents affecting the land registered after the effective date of the certificate and prior to the registration date of the certificate (the effective date being the date that the certification office completed its search);
(b) particulars of documents registered subsequent to the registration date of the certificate and to the registration date of the plan;
(c) particulars of documents referred to in the schedule of encumbrances of the certificate;
(d) particulars of the certificate number, time and date.

A review of the Patent document for reservations or easements is unusual but a few solicitors request it.

Of course, mortgages, liens and agreements which are subsequently discharged or released need only to be abstracted — not read.

Moreover, where lots are excepted from the certificate, a search should be made of the excepted part. It does not mean that title defects exist, but there was probably insufficient information to certify the title.

Prior to January, 1977 a paper print of the plan prepared in support of the application under the Certification of Titles Act was attached to the Certificate of Titles (CTA) and copies were available only from the examiners of surveys office. They are now deposited as reference plans under Part II of the Registry Act and their number is incorporated into Schedule A of the certificate of title. The land is described by reference to PARTS and copies are available from the Land Registrar.

RE-ABSTRACTING OF DOCUMENTS PRIOR TO PLAN OF SUBDIVISION

A new and welcome procedure was adopted under the Registry Act, R.S.O. 1970, c. 409, s. 82(1) [now R.S.O. 1980, c. 445, s. 78(1)] which gives the Director of Land Registration authority to direct Land Registrars to include an abstract of all documents affecting the land to be subdivided, in the abstract of the plan book immediately preceding the pages opened for lots on the new plan. This procedure became effective June 16, 1978, and also applies to lots that have been further subdivided, s. 78(2).

REVIEW OF TITLE SEARCH

Finally, a brief of your review of the search should be prepared to facilitate the solicitor in preparing requisitions.

Summary of Title Search Dated

Registry — Land Titles — POLARIS — PIN —
Cert. of Title —
Lot — Plan — Munic'ty — City — Town —
Parcel — Section —
R-plan — Sevr'nce — Imperial — Metric —
Page — Reg'd. owner and no.—
Page — Easement no.—
Page — Last reg'd doc. no.—
Page — Abutting land search—
Page — Execution search — Date — Clear —
Page — Agrt. no.—
Page — Rest'ns no. —
Page — By-law no.—
Page — Encumbrances no.—

Suggested requisitions

CHAPTER 4

REGISTERED DOCUMENTS

REGISTRATION

Under the Registry system, registration constitutes notice to all persons claiming any interest in land subsequent to registration. While registration is not necessary to make a document effective, it is necessary to protect the interest of a client in a conveyance or other dealings with land against subsequent dealing or conveyances.

Documents are registered once they have been accepted by the Land Registrar and the appropriate fee is paid. A registration number, the date and the Land Registrar's certificate are stamped on each registered document and duplicate as evidence of registration.

Under the Land Titles system, documents are accepted, paid for and entered in the register if they are executed by the party recorded on the register as the registered owner. The L.R.R.A., 1984 provides for storage of documents in a computer index, so when a document is presented for registration, the registration clerk activates the counter computer terminal and checks the land description and the registered owner displayed on the screen. If they are identical, the document is stamped with the Land Registrar's stamp and registration number. Particulars from the document are then typed on the keyboard and subsequently displayed on the screen.

NEW DOCUMENT FORMS

Significant changes to the traditional documents presented for registration were legislated by the L.R.R.A., 1984 and became effective on April 1, 1985, O. Reg. 35/38.

The prescribed forms were standardized, shortened and designed in box format. They are expected to be used for all registrations; however Land Registrars have the liberty at their discretion to permit registration of a document that is not entirely in accord with a particular form. After registration the forms and documents are microfilmed and, on completion, the original is destroyed.

The reference "document" replaces "instrument" now, and the use of the corporate seal is optional. If not used, the signatories must state that they had the authority to bind the corporation.

Affidavits

Most of the affidavits found in old documents have been eliminated. The Affidavit of Residence and Value of the Consideration is still around, and specific affidavits which apply to Sale Papers, Court Orders and Transmission Applications.

Parties

In the past, parties to a document were described by their surname and at least one given name in full. From now on they must be described by their surname, first name and another given name, both in full. Evidence is not required to prove that a party has no middle name, and a document will not be refused under the circumstances. All additional given names are permitted to be used.

Moreover, a transfer/deed in favour of a partnership or the name under which one carries on business must indicate the names of the partners, while a corporation may continue to take title in its legal name.

These amendments assist in compiling a list of owners' names, so that in the future a writ of execution may be filed on title. For the same reason, the transferee's birthdate is also required.

Under the Registry Act, R.S.O. 1980, c. 445, a title searcher should check the parties with the prior registered document, and as in the past they must be identical.

Land Descriptions

Metes and bounds descriptions and easements are referred to in the new forms by reference to the registration number of the most recent deed transfer describing the same land. Where a plan or sketch is appended to the schedule, a statement is required that the document description is the same as the drawing.

Forms

A remarkable amount of time may be saved by title searchers and registration clerks when checking the new forms for compliance with the Acts. The box format provides for a mark with an "X" or a short statement and where box space is insufficient additional information may be added by schedule.

The forms are described as follows:

Form 1 — Transfer/deed — It is a document dealing with a freehold or leasehold conveyance of land and replaces the traditional deed and transfer. It comprises 17 boxes and a schedule for additional parties, consents, signatures, *etc.*

Schedule, *Form* 5 may be appended for additional information, plans, sketches and exclusion, or variation of covenants. Of particular importance are the following statements:

1. Provisions under s. 49 of the Planning Act, 1983, S.O. 1983, c. 1, that are incorporated into boxes 13 and 14. They should be signed and dated by the transferor, the transferor's solicitor and the transferee's solicitor. However, signing is optional and if the boxes are not completed, or partly completed, a document will not be refused by the Land Registrar. Note should be made as to whether or not the option was observed.
2. Provisions under the Family Law Act, 1986, S.O. 1986, c. 4, as to spousal status, age, matrimonial home and consent incorporated into boxes 8 and 9 should be executed by the transferor and dated.

Form 2 — Charge/mortgage — It is a lien for payment of a debt or other obligation and replaces the old mortgage and charge. The document contains 18 boxes and usually an appended schedule for additional provisions, plans, sketches, and exclusion or variation of covenants. Evidence of the following should be recorded on a search of title:

1. The standard charge terms registration number (institutional lenders' loans) from box 8, or the payment provisions provided by other lenders and inserted in box 9.
2. A statement of compliance with the Family Law Act, 1986 as to spousal status, age, matrimonial home and consent in boxes 11 and 12. It should be executed and dated.

Form 3 — Discharge of Charge/Mortgage — There are ten boxes which should be completed with an "X" or short statement. The statements are quite explicit and contain the same requirements as in the former discharge of mortgage and cessation of charge.

Form 4 — Document General — It comprises 15 boxes and attached schedules for use when there is insufficient space in the boxes. It is used for registration of all documents except transfers, charges and discharges of charges.

Form 5 — Schedule — There are no boxes to check, just a blank page for additional information, descriptions, parties, executions, *etc.,* and it may be attached to the document form.

DOCUMENTS PRIOR TO APRIL 1, 1985

Documents registered under the Land Titles Act, R.S.O. 1980, c. 230, do not require reviewing for compliance with the Acts unless for some reason it becomes necessary. However, under the Registry Act, R.S.O. 1980, c. 445, they must be reviewed; also lands which have been designated to the L.R.R.A., 1984 still require a 40 year search prior to the designation date so the following documents require a review as in the past.

Deed or Transfer

The legal estate in land passed by deed under the Registry system or transferred under the Land Titles system. They were at one time also referred to as a grant, a conveyance or an indenture of bargain and sale.

Deeds and transfers registered prior to the new forms should be checked for the following:

(a) The Act under which it was made.

(b) The date of the document and of registration.

(c) A full description of the parties of the first part, second part, *etc.*, and the relationship between them, where given. For practical reasons the parties to a document are referred to on the search as one and two throughout, *e.g.*, one grants to two, three releases interest.

(d) Recitals.

(e) The consideration as set out in the Affidavit of Residence and of Value of the Consideration.

(f) The granting clause — the grantor grants to the grantee in fee simple (which means that he holds the absolute interest in the lands for himself and his heirs) as joint tenants, tenants in common, as partnership property, or in trust. When there is no recital it is considered that they take as tenants in common.

(g) A full description of the land including easements or rights of way that it is subject to.

(h) Four covenants and release of claim.

(i) Subject to the reservations, limitations, provisos, and conditions expressed in the original grant from the Crown, means that the deed is subject to the reservations in the Crown Patent.

(j) Bar of Dower — Execution by the wife is sufficient evidence of her release.

(k) *Habendum* — Recital of covenants, conditions or restrictions running with the land or purporting to be annexed thereto are recited in this clause. Make copies of any that have not expired.

Vendor's liens for the outstanding purchase price by way of a mortgage are also reserved herein. Establish whether or not the mortgage is discharged.

(l) Execution by the grantor or anyone releasing interest and by the grantee to observe covenants.

(m) The following affidavits are required:

   (i) Affidavit of execution;

   (ii) Affidavit of age and spousal status; see check list for dates;

   (iii) A combined Affidavit of Residence and of Value of the Consideration became mandatory May 1, 1979 replacing the old Affidavits of Residence and Land Transfer Tax;

   (iv) Affidavit of the Planning Act;

   (v) Affidavit of Land Speculation Tax was in effect from April 10, 1974 to October 24, 1978.

Particulars of the affidavits will be found in Chapter 6. Make notes of any of the above items that are missing, misspellings of names, handwritten alterations and lines typed over.

Where recitals relating to statements, facts, *etc.*, *i.e.*, that the grantor is a widower or that a joint tenant has died, in deeds, deposits or other documents are 20 years old, you have sufficient proof of the truth — you need not search for further evidence.

Transfers do not require checking, unless, of course, for particulars of restrictions, or covenants that the register indicated are in existence.

The forms for deeds and transfers were completely revised in 1979 and reduced to three pages.

The specific details in a deed must be recorded on your search, so a stamp, embossed with an abbreviated check list, saves time. The following, although abbreviated, are readily recognizable and should be checked off where applicable:

S.F.C.A	S.F.M.A.
D.E.A.	E.A.A.
F.S. HAB.	J.T.　　　　TIC. Uses Part'ship. prp'ty. Trustee　　　As trustee
COV. (4)-(1) rel.	
B. Dow. — to 31-3-78, except prior vested int.	
Aff.	M. Stat. — 25-6-39 to 31-3-78 SP. Stat. — 31-3-78 to 4-1-85 Age — 25-6-39 to 4-1-85 L.T.T. (V.&C.) — 1-6-21 Mort'n. — Ont. co. — 30-4-54 to 23-4-65 　　　　　Que. co. — 30-4-54 to 15-4-82
S.S.	C.S.
Statm't. — Part'ship. prpty. (3)	
Cons.	Ont. — 1-1-70 to 10-4-79 Fed. — forgiven Plan'g. Act — 15-6-67
Des'n. O.K.	
Sol.	

L.R.R.A., 1984 —	Reg. O. —　　　　　　L.T.O. —
Form — 1　2　3　4	Sched. —
Des'n. — 　　　　　PIN — 　　　　Pages —	
Interest/Este. —	
Statm't.	Birth date transferor —
	Spouse — Yes　No
	Spouse each other —
	Mat. home — Yes　No
	Sep'n. agrt. —
	Ct. order re: mat. home — Yes　No
	Not desig'd. mat. home. s. 41, F.L.R.A. —
	Doc. authorized s. 44, F.L.R.A. —
Sig.	Transferor — 　　and sol. —
	Transferee's sol. —

Executor / Administrator's Deed

Such a deed performs basically the same function as a regular deed, as personal representative of the deceased. They are subject to the Estates Administration Act, R.S.O. 1980, c. 143, formerly the Devolution of Estates Act, and should contain the following:

1. Recitals relating to the purpose of the sale which should be recorded with caution.
2. Bar of dower of the widow where applicable.
3. The legatees join to release their interest.
4. The Official Guardian approves on behalf of infants.
5. The signature of the Executor or Administrator as the personal representative of the deceased, and his or her capacity should be noted after the signature. Also, when he releases a personal interest, and at that time only, an affidavit of age and spousal status is required by him.
6. Registration particulars of the Will and the Ontario Succession Duty Consent prior to April 10, 1979 and Federal Estate Consents prior to December 31, 1971. A search of the General Register Index will fill you in on this information if the deed does not. Details of the particulars to be noted from Wills are described in the section related thereto.

Confirmation that a person is dead is usually provided by an affidavit or a death certificate.

Recitals often required confirmation that they were true and there was usually a statutory declaration to that effect deposited on title or an affidavit on the affidavit of execution form or, on the new documents, a statement prepared on schedule Form 5.

The payment of debts of a deceased is a lien against land specifically devised to an heir or heirs, or upon it becoming part of the residence of the estate. The debt must be paid, or the land released from the lien, s. 5 of the Act.

A purchaser may get title free from debts in the following cases:

1. Where a Will contains an express power of sale or an implied power, which is a direction to the executors to pay debts, a statutory declaration declaring that the debts of the estate have been paid and that the sale of the property is for that purpose should be provided.
2. Where an Executor or an Administrator states that the deed is given for the purpose of paying the debts.
3. Where an Executor or an Administrator states that the deed is for the purpose of distribution and the majority of the persons entitled to the land join in the deed.

Dealing with the person beneficially entitled to the land under the Will often creates a problem. Land vests in such a person three years after the death of the deceased person whether or not a deed has been registered.

The executor or administrator may register a caution on title which will postpone vesting for a further three years and enable him to pay the debts and dispose of assets.

Similarly, with an administrator's deed, the administrator has three years to pay the debts of the deceased, but if he has not registered a deed to the persons beneficially entitled thereto at the end of that time the land vests in such persons. In that case a statement is required by the persons dealing with the land that they are the widow and six children, and that there are no other children.

However, property will not vest until the Ontario Succession Duty and the Federal Estate Tax consents have been registered prior to the dates aforementioned.

Lands held as joint tenants by two persons are not dealt with under a Will. Title automatically passes to the survivor. The deed from the surviving joint tenant will recite the death of the other joint tenant and that he is the owner by right of survivorship. Succession duty consents are not required where real property interests pass by the law of survivorship. If the survivor was the spouse of the deceased, an affidavit to that effect was included with the affidavit of age and marital status prior to the new documents. Now a statement is required.

Under the Land Titles system it is much less complicated for the searcher. A transmission application is made registering the title in the executor's or administrator's name. However, where the Will does not provide for an express or an implied power of sale, the land vests in the beneficiary, who may apply directly to the Land Registrar after three years to be entered on the register as the owner.

The Public Trustee

The Public Trustee is the committee for the mentally incompetent person under the Mental Health Act, R.S.O. 1980, c. 262, s. 38. Where real estate is involved, the committee has the power to sell or otherwise deal with the land, subject to the approval of the court. A certified copy of the Court Order is registered on title and the searcher should examine it and make notes of the powers granted. Particulars of the Order should also be recited in the deed and the Public Trustee's consent endorsed thereon.

The Official Guardian

An Official Guardian is appointed by the provincial government to protect the interests of, administer property and concur in the sale of property devised an infant (anyone under 18 years as of September 1, 1971) in a Will, or left to a trustee in trust, unless the trustee has been given the express power in the Will to sell the property.

Deed to Uses

A deed to uses was a device to avoid a wife's right to dower in her husband's land. Dower was abolished under the Family Law Reform Act on March 31, 1978. However, outstanding dower interests prior to that date must be accounted for. A discharge or mortgage registered prior to a husband selling his land has the effect of vesting the legal estate free from uses making the land subject to dower. A careful check should be made for such discharges. In the deed or transfer, "to uses" replaces "fee simple" and the granting clause "grants and appoints" when selling.

Quit Claim Deed

It is a release of any claim or interest which a person may have in land registered under the Registry system. A mortgagee may quit claim the equity of redemption to the mortgagor when a mortgage is in default. Record particulars as in a regular deed.

Tax Deed

The tax deeds and tax arrears certificates registered on title prior to the introduction of the forms provided by the L.R.R.A., 1984 were brief. They provided a concise description of the land, the parties, statutory declaration and the Act, all of which should be recorded on title. Form 1 is now used for a tax deed and a tax arrears certificate. Form 4, Document General, is required for statutory declarations regarding notices and tax arrears cancellation certificates.

Grant Under Power of Sale

It is identical to any other grant except that it contains recitals as to the sale which are:

1. the registration date and number of the mortgage, and of the assignment if applicable;
2. provision on default of payment that the mortgagee may on 30 days' notice enter and sell the land;
3. that default occurred.

The granting clause differs in that it grants by virtue of the power of sale and all other powers enabling them to grant in fee simple, *etc.*

Under the Land Titles Act foreclosure proceedings under a charge are identical to those under a mortgage. An application is made to register the chargee as the owner. His or her title will be made subject to all prior encumbrances, unless an encumbrance having apparent priority is specifically debarred in the foreclosure order.

Memorials of Indenture of Bargain and Sale were registered in the past century. They recite the parties and the land as in a deed; also an affidavit by the witness to the signature of the party of the first part, that he saw the Indenture to which the Memorial related signed by the party of the first part and that he was a witness to the execution of the Indenture.

FINAL ORDER OF FORECLOSURE

Failure to make mortgage payments as provided in a mortgage results in the mortgagee issuing a Final Order of Foreclosure against the mortgagor, and other registered encumbrancers.

Subsequently, the Order is registered on title, and if the property is not redeemed within a time period set by the courts, the mortgagee becomes the registered owner of the property.

MORTGAGE AND CHARGE

A mortgage was a pledging of property to a creditor as security for the payment of a debt. The creditor (mortgagee) then held title to the land, subject to the owner's (mortgagor's) right to redeem (the equity of redemption) the land upon payment of the principal and interest.

Not so under the L.R.R.A., 1984, which provides that a charge/mortgage does not transfer a legal estate in land; it creates only a security interest which is discharged on payment of the principal and interest.

A complete 40 year search of title is required to establish whether or not the mortgagor is the registered owner of the lands and what prior encumbrances exist.

Prior to the 1940s almost all mortgages or charges were repaid quarterly, principal plus interest. Today most mortgages are paid by monthly installments and the term for repayment is five years; at that time the balance due is owing, *e.g.,* a mortgage for $12,000.00 with repayments of $100.00 monthly over a five year term will require a balance payment of $6,000.00 at the end of the term.

The current trend is toward a term of less than five years because of the fluctuating interest rates.

Amortization means the length of time that it would take for a mortgage to be paid in full at the end of the term, *e.g.,* a mortgage for $12,000.00 with payments of $100.00 plus interest would be amortized over a period of 10 years. There would not be a large balance or balloon payment, as it is referred to, owing to the mortgage at the end of the term.

Types of Mortgages

1. *Building and Completion Loan* — A mortgage referred to as a building loan is different, in that advances are made as construction proceeds. The title should be subsearched and executions searched against the builder immediately prior to each advance. The solicitor holds the cheque for the advance until he is advised that the builder still owns the land and that no mechanics' liens or charges/mortgages have been registered since the last advance. On completion of construction, with the lender's approval, the full amount of the loan is advanced.

2. *Purchase Money Charge/Mortgage* — When the vendor takes a mortgage as security for payment of the balance of the purchase price, it is commonly referred to as a charge/mortgage back. A vendor's lien should be reserved in the deed for the outstanding balance of the purchase price, which lien is to be collaterally secured by a charge/mortgage, and the registration of a discharge of the charge/mortgage shall operate as a discharge of the lien.

3. *Bond Charge/Mortgage or Trust Deeds* — These charges/mortgages are usually for large sums of money and are given by the borrower to a trustee who holds title to the property in trust for several lenders who combine their monies to lend a portion of the total amount. On repayment the borrower is given a re-conveyance and a release and a standard form discharge of charge/mortgage is registered, particulars of which should be recorded on the search. Make sure that the correct corporate seal is affixed.

4. *Charge/Mortgage of a Charge/Mortgage* — A charge/mortgage of a charge/mortgage or a discharge thereof will not be registered without a judge's fiat from and after January 1, 1970. To charge a charge/mortgage as security for the repayment of monies advanced it should be done by way of an assignment of charge/mortgage which should contain a provision for reassignment to the assignor upon payment of the monies due. On repayment the charge/mortgage is reassigned to the original chargee/mortgagee.

5. *Blanket Charge/Mortgage* — This assists would-be purchasers where a low interest rate first charge/mortgage is registered. Sometimes lenders will provide a second charge/mortgage which will include the outstanding principal of the first. The second chargee/mortgagee will undertake to make payments to the first chargee/mortgagee to keep the first charge/mortgage in good standing.

6. *National Housing Act Charge/Mortgage* — This is a federal government scheme to assist housing development. The money is borrowed from

approved lenders and repayment is guaranteed by the Central Mortgage and Housing Corporation.

7. *Variable Rate Charge/Mortgage* — The answer to the problem of fluctuating interest rates is a loan where, if the rate declines, a larger payment on account of the principal will be due. If it increases so a monthly payment does not cover the accrued previous month's interest, then the shortfall will be added to the principal. The charger/mortgagor will owe more principal than he borrowed, and the lender gains by the inflation rate, increasing the value of the property.

8. *Chattel Mortgages and Conditional Sale Agreements* — Personal property, such as automobiles, televisions, stoves, refrigerators, *etc.*, is often held as security, and the security interest is registered under the Personal Property Security Act, R.S.O. 1980, c. 375, in the form of a chattel mortgage, a conditional sale agreement, or an equipment lease.

An agreement of purchase and sale for real property often includes the purchase of drapes, stoves, *etc.* In that case, a search of the records at the Personal Property Security Office at 393 University Ave., Third Floor, Toronto, Ontario, or a local district office, will provide a printout of registrations against the presumed owner. Previous owners should also be searched and the office will provide the names. A certified printout provides the right to claim against the P.P.S. assurance fund if information provided is incorrect. Searches by telephone are accepted provided the list is brief.

Assignment of Mortgage and Transfer of Charge

By an assignment of a charge/mortgage the mortgagee assigns the fee in the mortgaged land to the assignee and all his rights to collect the outstanding principal and interest. If the charge/mortgage has been discharged do not record its contents but note the particulars of the recitals, execution and affidavits. From and after January 1, 1970 the assignment may contain a provision for re-assignment to the original mortgagee upon payment of the debt.

Discharge of Mortgage and Cessation of Charge

A discharge of a mortgage on registration operated to vest the legal title in the mortgagor (the registered owner). Currently, a security interest created by the charge/mortgage, Form 2, is discharged on payment of the debt. The new Form 3, in use since April 1, 1985, replaces the old discharge form.

On registration of Form 3, the duplicate charge/mortgage, and assignments thereof, should be produced. If they are lost, a statement to that effect should be recited in box 7 of the form.

The following particulars from a discharge should be recorded:

1. the parties — they should identify with the parties to the mortgage;
2. the registration date and number of an assignment or re-assignment, or other document relating thereto, so the Land Registrar can rule them off the abstract book or the register;
3. recital to the effect that the mortgage is "discharged";
4. the description — required where a plan of subdivision has been registered on the land subsequent to the registration of the mortgage, the discharge must contain a description of the land as it is presently described, *e.g.,* lots 1 to 50 inclusive on Plan 8382, to assist the Land Registrar in abstracting the discharge on the land discharged;
5. execution and affidavits — a red seal is not required.

Ontario Regulation 637/79 provides that, as of January 1, 1980, a cessation of a charge requires a registrable description of the land to be discharged, whether the cessation is partial or complete. However, if the description is not available, you may make reference to the parcel against which the charge was originally registered, if that parcel still includes all the land affected by the charge.

Partial Discharge or Partial Cessation

They are given on request as the lots on a plan of subdivision or part of the original parcel are sold. A reference plan is not required, nor the registered duplicate or assignments thereof.

Outstanding Mortgages and Charges

Where a mortgage or a charge has not been discharged, has not merged in the fee, or is not to be discharged on closing, the following particulars should be recorded:

1. the Act — Short Forms of Mortgages Act, or Form 2 Land Registration Reform Act, 1984;
2. the date made and registered;
3. a description of the mortgagor, mortgagee and guarantor if there is one and their relationships. Also the wife of the mortgagor where she joins to bar her dower;
4. the description of the land;
5. dower — in a mortgage only operates to the extent necessary to give effect to the right of the mortgagee and dower rights are restored upon discharge of the mortgage;
6. details of the repayment clause;
7. provisions as to notice upon default;

8. privileges — they are not usually a part of the standard form and a copy should be made. An open mortgage contains the following privilege: "PROVIDED that the Mortgagor, when not in default hereunder, shall have the privilege of paying all or any part or parts of the principal sum hereby secured at any time or times, without notice or bonus";
other privileges are for additional payments on any interest date, renewal of the present mortgage, the mortgage due on a sale of the lands, partial discharges and demolition of buildings;
a bonus is an extra payment of interest required before the mortgagee will accept pre-payment of the principal before the due date;
9. the consent of the Committee of Adjustment, which is required when the mortgagor retains the fee in any abutting land;
10. execution, affidavits, and statements under L.L.R.A., 1984.

The guarantor guarantees payment in the event that the mortgagor fails to pay as is witnessed by his signature.

CONSTRUCTION LIEN

The Construction Lien Act, 1983, S.O. 1983, c. 6, repealed and replaced the Mechanics' Lien Act, R.S.O. 1980, c. 261, on April 2, 1983.

A construction lien is a lien in favour of a person who supplies services or materials relating to construction, repair or improvement, provided to an owner, contractor or subcontractor. The lien attaches to the interest of the owner in the premises improved. It gives the person the right, in addition to his ordinary creditor's rights, in certain circumstances, to sell the land and to apply the proceeds to his debts. The title searcher has to provide both the name of the registered owner and the legal description of the lands post haste, so the lien may be registered — often that day. Usually, the person has a street address, and in that case it is possible to establish the lot and plan number from the assessment maps provided by the Registry Office.

Where land is currently under development the most problems arise. You may be requested to locate the lot and plan number for an apartment building on a new street which is 1,000 feet north from the north west corner of Keele and Wilson Avenues. Again, the assessment maps will provide the necessary information.

It is most important that the lien be registered on the land where the work was performed. The description in the lien may be by reference to the registration number of a previously registered document, so you need not copy a long land description.

If the lien has not been discharged, the following should be recorded on your search:

1. name and address of parties;
2. when work was done and material supplied;
3. land description.

If payment is not made a lien claimant perfects his lien by commencing an action and by registering a certificate of action on title.

Finally, on payment, the court shall make an order vacating the registration of a claim for lien and certificate of action. The following information should be included on your search:

1. name and address of the parties which must identify with that in the lien;
2. evidence that the lien and action are discharged.

The new Form 4, Document General is used for the lien and the certificate of action.

NOTICE OF SECURITY INTEREST

A creditor who claims a security interest in a fixture may register a Notice of Security Interest in the land registration office to protect his rights under s. 54 of the Personal Property Security Act. Fixtures are chattels attached to a building in such a way that they become a part of the land.

Registration is good for five years; an extension may be registered on expiry and, on discharge, a Discharge of Notice of Security Interest is registered.

LIS PENDENS

The object of such a certificate is to warn would-be purchasers that there is a pending litigation which would affect the land. It is registered under the Registry system, and a caution is filed under the Land Titles system.

A certificate of a vacating order may be registered as a release of the land from the claims of the plaintiff.

DEPOSITS

Deposited in the Land Registry Office General Register Index are documents such as surveys and statutory declarations which verify facts recited in documents or clarify defects in title. Deposit of a document does not deem registration so it does not provide notice.

Prior to April 1, 1985 deposits were attached to a requisition which provided a description of the land and of the parties. Since that date, you will find them on Form 4, Document General.

They are indexed by number rather than by municipality, and should be requisitioned by number, "2634 Deposit." Prior to 1937 they were not abstracted on the title so you may find it necessary to search the alphabetical index. Record the following on your search:

1. all dates;
2. the statutes under which it was executed;
3. a concise summation of its contents or, if it is long, a copy.

NOTICE OF AGREEMENT OF PURCHASE AND SALE

The Registry Act, R.S.O. 1980, c. 445, s. 21(8) provides that a notice of agreement of purchase and sale, or an assignment thereof, or a notice of an option to purchase, or an assignment thereof, will expire one year after the date of its registration. When they are outstanding on title, record particulars of the parties, purchase price, terms and any clauses over and above the standard form.

LEASES

Under the Registry system a leasehold interest may be created by the execution of a lease, or an agreement for lease. Leases or notices exceeding seven years not registered on title are considered void against subsequent purchasers and mortgagees.

Under the Land Titles system, an application should be made to register a Notice of Lease, or of an agreement to lease on the register. If the term is in excess of 21 years (including any right of renewal), the lessee may apply to the Land Registrar to be registered as the owner of a leasehold title. An executed copy of the lease must form part of the application.

The following particulars should be recorded on your search:

1. the parties;
2. a description of the demised premises;
3. commencement date and term;
4. payments and dates;
5. renewal clause;
6. right to purchase the demised lands on termination of the lease;
7. any provisions typed other than the standard form;
8. proper execution.

A release may be registered under the Registry system and an application for a Notice of Determination of Lease under the Land Titles system.

LETTERS PROBATE AND ADMINISTRATION

Probate is the procedure by which the Surrogate Court approves a Will to be the valid last Will and Testament of the deceased and confirms the appointment of the person named in the Will as executor/trix.

After a Will has been probated in the Surrogate Court a notarial copy of the Letters Probate is registered in the General Registry of the Land Registry Office in which any land devised in the Will is situate.

The Will should be reviewed with particular regard to the disposition of the land and to charges it may be subject to. Record the following particulars:

1. In respect of the Probate:
   (i) the county and date of granting;
   (ii) the name, marital status and the date of the decease of the testator/ trix;
   (iii) the names of the executors appointed.
2. In respect of:
   (a) the Will and Codicil, if applicable;
   (b) Letters Double Probate or other grant to a personal representative based on a Will;
   (c) Letters of Administration with the Will annexed;
       (i) the devisor's name (should identify with the name on the deed);
       (ii) the executor appointed;
       (iii) any devisee in trust affecting the land being searched or specific devisee of the land;
       (iv) any charge, legacy or other reservation affecting the specific devisee of the land;
       (v) payment to a widow in lieu of her dower;
       (vi) power to sell the property or direction to pay debts.
3. In respect of Letters of Administration of the estate of an intestate:
   (i) the county;
   (ii) the intestate's name;
   (iii) the date of decease;
   (iv) the administrator appointed.
4. In respect of a grant of Probate or Administration made outside of Ontario to a personal representative:
   (i) the Court and its territorial jurisdiction.

When the registration number of a Will has not been recited in a deed or other instrument, search the General Register, commonly known as the G.R. index.

ENVIRONMENTAL PROTECTION ACT DOCUMENTS

Certificates of approval and provisional certificates of approval respecting waste management systems and waste disposal sites under Part V of the Environmental Protection Act, R.S.O. 1980, c. 141, and certificates of approval respecting private sewage disposal systems under Part VIII are registered under the Registry Act and a notice of certificate is registered under the Land Titles Act. Any restrictions or conditions in the certificate as to the use of the land should be recorded on your search of title.

SUCCESSION DUTY ACT

Where persons died between January 1, 1970 and April 10, 1979 the deed, mortgage or other instrument must have one of the following:

1. the Consent of the Treasurer of Ontario attached thereto, or endorsed thereon;
   or
2. that the original certificate and notarial copy be registered and the registration date and number recited in the document.

Such duty is a first lien and charge on the property until a certificate is given to discharge it.

The certificate should contain the following:

1. an abbreviated description or a reference to a registration number of a previously registered document;
2. the deceased should be described as in the document registered to him or her;
3. the date of death. When a mortgagee dies holding a mortgage, consent will be required.

FEDERAL ESTATE TAX ACT

An estate tax release was required for persons who died between January 1, 1959 and January 1, 1972. However, under an amendment to the Act, they are no longer required, and the Department of National Revenue will not issue a release for outstanding notices registered on title — in effect, they can be ignored.

NOTICE OF LIEN

Listing the names of corporate owners found in a chain of title is no longer necessary. Since 1979, the Minister of Revenue has registered a notice of lien on title for outstanding taxes against corporations. If the notice has not been discharged, record particulars of the corporation, the date and amount of the lien.

CORPORATE OWNERSHIP

Where title to land is registered in the name of a corporation, a searcher should establish whether or not it was an incorporated company at the time of purchase and of sale of the land.

Particulars of incorporation, the status of the company, and the date of dissolution, if that be the case, may be searched at the Corporate Search Office, 393 University Ave., Toronto, Ontario, or at the courthouse in smaller municipalities.

Moreover, you may find that a corporation has changed its name, and in that instance a notarial copy , or a certified copy of Articles of Amendment, will be on file in the General Register Index of the Registry Office. Under the Land Titles system, an application to amend the register (Form 4) is registered.

PARTNERSHIP PROPERTY

Two or more people may purchase land as partnership property. The granting clause of the deed must read, "in fee simple as partnership property," or, "as partners". Otherwise the land will be considered as being held as tenants in common. There was no dower interest in partnership property.

The deed from the partnership must be signed by all the partners and contain the following declaration, made by one of the partners:

1. the land was purchased as partnership land;
2. the land was held as partnership land up to the date of the sale;
3. the names of all the partners, and that they were the only partners in the partnership.

Executions should be searched against each member of the partnership and the name under which they carry on business.

Limited partnerships are uncommon; only the general partners are authorized to sign and their names are set forth in the declaration which is filed with the Registrar of Partnerships.

If you are requested to check the registration of a partnership or examine the declaration under the Partnerships Registration Act, R.S.O. 1980, c. 371, attend at the Ministry of Consumer and Commercial Relations, Registrar of Partnerships, Companies Division, 393 University Ave., Second Floor, Toronto. The declaration provides:

1. the names and addresses of all the parties;

2. the names and addresses under which they intend to carry on business;
3. their solicitors.

JOINT TENANCY AND TENANTS IN COMMON

Where land is conveyed to two or more persons they take title as tenants in common unless it is stated in the deed that they take as joint tenants. The undivided interest of each tenant is often expressed in the deed.

In a deed or will where title is taken as joint tenants each tenant has an equal share of the whole. The granting clause and the habendum recite as joint tenants and not as tenants in common. When one tenant dies the entire interest automatically passes to the surviving joint tenant or tenants. When the land is sold the deed from the surviving joint tenants should contain a recital to the effect that the land was held as joint tenants and they are granting by right of survivorship. A widow has no right to dower, nor can the interest be devised under a will.

TRUSTEE

The granting clause of a deed or mortgage may indicate that the land is to be held in trust, or as a trustee. It is usually done to avoid identity or land vesting in a minor. Trusts are unique to the Registry system.

VENDOR'S LIEN

Under the Registry Office system, when the balance of the monies due to the vendor on delivery of the deed to the purchaser is secured on terms, the vendor has a lien for unpaid purchase monies. It is referred to in the habendum of the deed and is a notice on title to subsequent purchasers and mortgagees of the land.

When it is secured by a mortgage given back to the vendor the recital in the deed is usually, "subject to a vendor's lien for unpaid purchase money to be secured by a mortgage in favour of John Smith and a discharge of the mortgage shall operate as a discharge of the lien". If the mortgage is not discharged the lien is outstanding and an encumbrance against the land.

When the terms of the lien are not specifically expressed in the deed it is discharged from title by a release.

Under the Land Titles system the lien may be registered by way of a caution and an application is made to remove it from title.

GENERAL REGISTRATION INDEX

Pursuant to R.S.O. 1980, c. 445, s. 18(6), the following documents, because they do not contain a land description, shall be registered as general registrations, and except as otherwise provided in this Act shall not be recorded in the abstract index. However, they can be requisitioned from the General Register Index, which contains the following documents:

1. wills;
2. letters probate;
3. letters of administration;
4. general appointments of new trustees;
5. certificates or certified or notarial copies of judgments or of court orders appointing or removing executors, administrators, guardians or trustees;
6. certificates or certified or notarial copies of orders made under the Mental Incompetency Act;
7. certificates under s. 19 of the Change of Name Act;
8. powers of attorney or revocation thereof;
9. general bars of dower;
10. orders in council of Canada or Ontario, or certified copies thereof, not containing local descriptions;
11. notarial copies of letters patent or certificates of incorporation, supplementary letters patent or certificates, or certificate of continuance;
12. notarial copies of letters patent or certificates changing names of corporations or amalgamating corporations;
13. notarial copies of certificates of amalgamation of loan or trust corporations;
14. notarial copies of licences in mortmain;
15. notarial copies of extra-provincial licences.

CHAPTER 5

THE FAMILY LAW REFORM ACT

The Family Law Reform Act, 1978, S.O. 1978, c. 2. s. 70(2) repealed the Dower Act and abolished a widow's right to dower, effective March 1, 1978, except for rights which had vested prior to that date. In the past, a wife barred dower by signing a deed or transfer; reference to it in the document was not necessary. Where she has not signed and her husband died prior to March 1, 1978, her interest will remain outstanding until she signs or until her decease.

The Act also provided a new Affidavit of Age and Marital Status form for inserting in documents, and it was known as the Affidavit of Age and Spousal Status. An authorization under the L.R.R.A., 1984, effective April 1, 1985, by O. Reg. 35/85, incorporated a statement into the new document forms, "I am a spouse" and "I am at least eighteen years old", to replace the Affidavit of Age and Spousal Status.

The Family Law Reform Act, R.S.O. 1980, c. 152 and the Family Law Act, 1986, S.O. 1986, c. 4 legislated more changes to the law of property and relationship between spouses.

As a practical matter, the spouse's property reference was changed to "the matrimonial home" and was defined as property that is or has been occupied by the person and his or her spouse as a matrimonial home. Once a property ceases to be used as such, the designation expires. Other properties may be designated by registering a designation, s. 20, Family Law Act, 1986. It must be signed by both spouses; otherwise, another property designated will remain a matrimonial home. Suffice to say that if only one spouse signs, make a note to that effect on your search.

A spouse's signature to a document is evidence of his or her consent to the transaction. Nevertheless, there are legal reasons for not signing and they are:

1) grantor/mortgagor was not a spouse;
2) the property was never occupied as a matrimonial home;
3) another property was designated under s. 4 as the matrimonial home;

4) spouse released all his or her rights by a written separation agreement.

An unsigned document should provide a statement containing one of the above reasons.

Title should be checked for dower rights which vested prior to March 31, 1978 except in the following instances where dower did not arise or was avoided:

1. lands held as joint tenants;
2. lands held as partnership property;
3. lands held as trustee;
4. lands in the state of nature;
5. an equitable estate — the mortgagor holds only the equity of redemption, so dower would not attach until the mortgage is discharged and he could sell the land in the interim without his wife joining to bar her dower;
6. lands dedicated as streets and public highways;
7. divorce — affidavit of marital status will indicate that he is divorced;
8. adultery — where wife goes off with adulterer;
9. insanity — where wife confined to a mental hospital when husband purchased lands;
10. where a wife has not lived in Ontario since her marriage;
11. where husband and wife are living apart and her whereabouts are unknown;
12. a deed to uses;
13. sale of land for taxes;
14. widow's benefit in her husband's Will accepted in lieu of dower;
15. the lapse of ten years from the husband's death: the Limitations Act, R.S.O. 1980, c. 240, s. 25;
16. where a man purchased land subject to a mortgage before marrying, then sold subject to the same mortgage, his spouse would have no dower interest in that land.

There are exceptions to these rules under the Land Titles Act, R.S.O. 1980, c. 230, s. 119, but since it is not necessary to check documents in that office there is no need to record them here.

CHAPTER 6

AFFIDAVITS

EXECUTION

The requirements for affidavits and the forms used in documents presented for registration have changed considerably throughout the years. The most significant change was in the elimination of them all except the Affidavit of Residence and of Value of the Consideration under L.R.R.A., 1984 legislation.

However, the affidavits included in documents registered prior to April 1, 1985, the effective date for the new legislation, should be checked, as in the past. Variances in the name or names on the affidavit and that of the party or parties to the document should be recorded on your search of title.

The signature on a document may be written in:

1. foreign characters;
2. signed by making his/her mark;
3. by recital that he/she was unable to read the document plus a statement made by a witness that he/she saw the individual sign the document after it had been read to him/her;
4. or even signed by initials that bear no significance to the name as set out in the document.

The main concern was that it had been properly witnessed and that the affidavit had been properly executed. The signature of public officials such as an Official Guardian does not require an affidavit.

Documents, other than a discharge of a mortgage presented for registration under the Registry system, required that a seal be affixed opposite the parties' signatures. This requirement was unique to the Registry system and, effective April 1, 1985, it was dispensed with.

Space was provided in the affidavit of execution for the insertion of a statement in respect to the residence of the vendor for the purpose of the Income Tax Act (Canada) (a declaration to that effect is now provided by the vendor on closing), also, for the declaration in respect to recitals — "the recitals herein are true." In the past, other important recitals were included in the affidavits, so title searchers should check old documents accordingly.

AFFIDAVITS SWORN OUTSIDE OF ONTARIO

The affidavits on a document sworn outside of Ontario, in another province or another country, were required to be sworn before one of the following:

1. a notary public who affixed his official seal to the document;
2. the head of a municipality who affixed the seal of the municipality to the document and noted his office below his signature;
3. an officer of Her Majesty's diplomatic or consular services who affixed the seal of his office on the document;
4. a commissioned officer, on full time service in the Canadian Forces, who noted his rank and unit below his signature.

Section 46(1)(d) of the Canada Evidence Act also provided that such affidavit be sworn before "a commissioner for taking affidavits" without any further evidence of such commissioner's capacity.

EXECUTION BY A CORPORATION

Before enactment of the L.R.R.A, 1984, a corporation executed documents by affixing its corporate seal over the signatures of its signing officers. A witness to the signatures was not required, but the office held was indicated below the signatures. The name on the corporate seal had to be identical to that set out in the document, *e.g.*, R.G. Simpson and Company Limited. The party to the document could not be R.G. Simpson & Co., Limited, on the seal. Even a missing comma or a period could nullify a document.

Where a corporate seal was missing on a document executed by a foreign corporation, an affidavit as evidence that a seal was not required in the jurisdiction where the corporation was incorporated had to be attached; also necessary was an affidavit with respect to the signing officers.

Finally, another provision of the L.R.R.A., 1984 was that use of the corporate seal was optional. If not used, the document must indicate the signatories' authority to sign.

AFFIDAVIT OF AGE

Anyone who executed a document completed an affidavit that he was of the full age of 18 years, except in the following cases:

1. a wife signing to bar her dower, and
2. an Executor, or an Administrator, the Public Trustee or any other Trustee, or the Official Guardian.

The new forms provide space for the transferor or chargor to certify that the transferor or chargor is at least 18 years old.

AFFIDAVIT OF MARITAL STATUS

Prior to the Family Law Reform Act which came into effect March 31, 1978 a widow had a right to dower in her husband's lands. A husband executed a document and made an affidavit that he:

1. was married, unmarried, divorced or widowed;
2. the man *or* the wife completed the affidavit that they were married at the time of execution of the document when the wife joined to bar her dower.

The affidavit was exempt in the following cases:

1. land held as joint tenants;
2. land held as trustees;
3. land held as partnership property;
4. execution as an executor or administrator of an estate.

When a person acted in his personal capacity as well as in his capacity as an executor or an administrator, the affidavits of age and marital status were required.

Meanwhile, blanks in the new forms provide space for the transferor/chargor to include a spousal status statement and a consent to the transaction.

AFFIDAVIT OF RESIDENCE AND OF VALUE OF THE CONSIDERATION

Under the Land Transfer Tax Act, R.S.O. 1980, c. 231, all transfer/deeds offered for registration must have an Affidavit of Residence and of Value of the Consideration attached. You will find documents on title where it was referred to as the Land Transfer Tax Affidavit and prior to that the Affidavit of Residence.

The Act provides that a tax, payable to the Treasurer of Ontario, based on the consideration recited in the document was due on tendering a document for registration. Also, an executed copy, or a copy of the original, should be left with the Land Registrar for forwarding to the Treasurer. It may be sworn by the purchaser, the purchaser's solicitor or an agent authorized in writing to act in their stead.

Prior to the L.R.R.A, 1984 the affidavit was sworn by one of the following:

1. each transferee or on their behalf by an agent authorized in writing to do so, or by their solicitor;
2. where the transferee happens to be a corporation, an officer thereof;
3. by one spouse on behalf of both;
4. where there is more than one transferee the affidavit may be severally sworn, provided they are entitled to mark the same square in para. 1 thereof.

Lawyers are usually interested in the consideration disclosed in the affidavit or any additional remarks relating to title.

Where a deed or transfer bears the stamp, "Land Transfer Tax paid by the Treasurer of Ontario receipt No. 2341," the consideration paid is not disclosed. However, it may be obtained by writing to or attending at the office of the Minister of Revenue, Land Transfer Section, 33 King Street West, Oshawa, Ontario and providing the following:

1. a written request to the Minister;
2. a copy of the deed or transfer, or particulars of registration, the parties and a description of the lands;
3. the receipt number.

AFFIDAVIT OF LAND SPECULATION TAX

This Affidavit was short-lived, becoming effective on April 10, 1974, and being repealed on October 24, 1987. If it is not attached to the document, it is not necessary to make notes to that effect.

POWERS OF ATTORNEY

For various reasons attorneys are appointed to execute documents on behalf of others. Of particular interest to title searchers is the donor's authorization to sell real estate and execute documents relating thereto.

The original power of attorney, or a copy, should be registered in the General Register Index of the office where the land is registered. The registration number and date of the power should be recited in the deed, or other document executed thereunder. If it is not, a search of the General Register Index should provide it. A search in that index should always be made, to determine if the power was revoked prior to the registration date of the document executed thereunder.

Once the power of attorney document is executed and witnessed, the attorney provides a statement (formerly an affidavit) that to the best of his knowledge and belief the power was in force and effect and not revoked, the donor was at least 18 years old, and the witness to his signature was not the attorney or the attorney's spouse.

One final note: The power automatically terminates on the death of the donor, or where the donor is declared mentally incompetent, or where the Public Trustee becomes the committee for the estate and upon appointment of a committee.

Designation of attorneys for banks differs considerably from that for individuals or other corporations. Bank managers are usually authorized to conduct business on behalf of the bank, but because of frequent staff transfers it would be impractical to register powers of attorney every time a transfer occurred. Accordingly, Land Registrars will register a power of attorney that designates the office or position held in the bank but does not name the individual. An affidavit of a subscribing witness must be attached to the document deposing that the person executing the document was authorized to do so as an attorney.

CHARITIES ACCOUNTING ACT

The Mortmain and Charitable Uses Act (Ontario) was repealed, effective June 15, 1982, and was replaced by an amendment to the Charities Accounting Act, R.S.O. 1980, c. 65, which permits charities to hold land subject to the right of the Public Trustee to register a notice vesting the land in himself, for the purpose of selling it, if he finds the land had not been used as a charity for three years and is no longer required for that purpose.

RELIGIOUS ORGANIZATIONS' LANDS ACT

Religious organizations are authorized to acquire land for specific purposes under the direction of the Religious Organizations' Lands Act, R.S.O. 1980, c. 448. The land is to be held in the name of trustees appointed by the organization and title vests automatically, only where successor trustees have not been appointed, and after existing trustees have all left office, s. 3(4),(5) and (6).

Trustees may only act upon the resolution of the organization. A certified copy of it should be deposited on title so title searchers can establish the exact authority granted the trustees.

CHAPTER 7

EXECUTIONS

REGISTRY OFFICE SYSTEM

An execution filed in the Sheriff's Office of the county or judicial district where the land is situated creates a lien against the land owned by the person named in the execution at and after the time of filing. Therefore, on completion of a search of title under the Registry Act a search of executions is required against the registered owner and his predecessors on title. There is nothing more annoying than to find at the last minute, on closing day, that executions were not searched, or that the search did not cover the entire 40 year period, particularly if the sheriff cannot give you a clear certificate.

Outstanding executions must be removed prior to closing a transaction or satisfactory proof be received from the execution creditor that the debtor is not one of the parties who had an interest in the lands at or after the date of the execution.

Particulars of an execution may be obtained on attendance at the Sheriff's Office, which is located in the county court house. The Toronto office at 361 University Avenue is for filing writs and the searches are carried out at 40 Dundas Street West, Fourth Floor, in the same building as the land registration offices. Usually, offices will acknowledge telephone requests, particularly if it is not a busy period.

When you are advised of an identical execution, *e.g.*, John James a former owner and John James the judgment debtor, you often find that they are not one and the same person. The vendor's solicitor should provide a statutory declaration to this effect and deposit it on title. The solicitor who filed the execution will provide you with the necessary information to prove that they are not one and the same.

A similar execution is where John Ashford is registered as the owner and the Sheriff's Office presents an execution against a John J. Ashford. Again, a statutory declaration solves the problem.

A writ filed against James Harris in August 1970 would not affect land he had sold in January 1960.

When the vendor is taking a mortgage back, it is no longer necessary to search executions against the new purchasers prior to closing, but most solicitors search because a purchaser money charge has priority over an execution creditor of purchaser-chargor-mortgagor.

The sheriff's certificate can no longer be brought up to date immediately prior to closing. On busy closing days such as the fifteenth and the end of the month it is advisable to go directly to the Sheriff's Office.

A search of executions for amalgamated or annexed lands is necessary in the county or provisional judicial district of which it was formerly a part, and in the bailiwick of the sheriff of which it is now a part, *e.g.*, part of the Township of Pickering was annexed to the Corporation of the Borough of Scarborough on January 1, 1974 so a search is essential at the Sheriff's Office at Whitby, in the County of Durham, and at Toronto, in the County of York until such time as each writ of execution is withdrawn, expired or renewed. In this case a writ at Whitby would have expired January 1, 1980.

Finally, there is a list of executions in the Sheriff's Office older than 40 years which also must be checked.

A writ may be renewed from time to time notwithstanding any period of limitation. Occasionally, you will find deposited on title a statutory declaration by a former registered owner that he is not the person named in a particular execution filed with the sheriff. However, the number differs from the one presented to you by the Sheriff's Office. That is because when a writ of execution is renewed, as required every six years, it is assigned a new number.

LAND TITLES SYSTEM

Under the Land Titles system the only executions that affect a parcel of land are those filed in that office by the sheriff. An execution certificate should be ordered just prior to presenting a document for registration. The counter clerk will complete the box provided on the new forms for executions, with an O.K. If the document is otherwise in order, it will be registered.

A copy of the writ of execution is filed in the Land Titles Office so, when you are advised there is an execution against the registered owner, you may get particulars of it in that office.

It is not necessary to search against prior owners, but it is advisable to order a certificate against the present registered owner(s) on completion of your land search. Thus, the problems created by finding an execution on presentation of a document on closing day are avoided. You may, of course, be advised by your office to register subject to an execution. In that case, the Land Registrar will make the following note on the register, "subject to execution number —".

Under the Land Titles system, as of December 17, 1981, to clear a writ of execution where the value of the writ is $10,000.00 or more, Land Registrars may now accept a letter from the solicitor for the registered owner, on the solicitor's letterhead, setting out the particulars required in the *Land Titles Procedural Guide*, p. 16-4 in lieu of a statutory declaration by the solicitor. The evidence must be explicit. It cannot be a general statement. Of course, the statutory declaration of the solicitor as set out on p. 16-4 will still be acceptable to clear a writ as well as a written acknowledgement by the judgment creditor or his solicitor.

CHAPTER 8

By-laws, Agreements and Covenants

RESTRICTIVE COVENANTS

Restrictive covenants were common on title prior to zoning by-laws. They restrict the land to certain uses for the benefit of the neighbourhood and usually run with the land for a defined period of time. Some of them may be modified or discharged by an order of a judge of the Supreme Court. Of course, there is no need to record details if they have expired.

Under the Land Titles system, it was the practice to delete them from the parcel register by making an application to do so when they had expired by at least 10 years or when they had been registered for 40 years or more, or where they did not contain an expiry date.

However, the Land Titles Act, R.S.O. 1980, c. 230, s. 118(9), provides that as of January 1, 1980 the condition, restriction or covenant is deemed to have expired after 40 years. Therefore the Land Registrar, on request, may delete them from the register without an application having been made and without payment of a fee.

They are registered under the Land Titles system in a transfer, or by making application to annex restrictive covenants to the land, and they are released by making application to register notices of their releases.

Under the Registry system they may be registered separately or in a deed and on performance a release is registered.

S. 22 of the Conveyancing and Law of Property Act, R.S.O. 1980, c. 90, voids restrictions made after March 24, 1950 that restrict ownership of land because of race, creed, colour, religion, nationality or place of origin.

Zoning and building by-laws, usually referred to as land use control by-laws, provide set back requirements from the street and side and rear lot allowance. If you have been provided with a survey, check for variances. Their chief function is to divide municipalities into specific areas and to designate land and building uses.

AIRPORT ZONING BY-LAWS

Airport zoning by-laws control the height of the buildings within a certain radius of an airport. The permitted height increases as the distance from the end of the runway increases. The document registered on title contains a large, complex map. Out of curiosity, you may wish to unfold it, but it will not be to your benefit to do so. Record only the particulars from the abstract book on your search. The Federal Department of Transport by whom it was registered no longer replies to enquiries. However, Ontario land surveyors are qualified to provide maximum height requirements.

SUBDIVISION AGREEMENTS

The requirements for such agreements differ from municipality to municipality. If a release has not been registered on title, check occupancy restrictions, zoning, written approvals required from the engineer and architect, monies required to be paid, the bond and discharge privileges for individual lots. Licence agreements are also registered to permit entry upon the lands to comply with the subdivision agreement until such time as the municipality accepts the subdivision.

Under the Land Titles system one makes application to register a Notice of Agreement and an application to register a Notice of Compliance on performance of the obligations. An agreement and a release thereof is registered under the Registry system.

CHAPTER 9

THE PLANNING ACT

The history of the Planning Act has been one of amendments since it was legislated in 1946. S. 29(2) enabled municipalities to pass by-laws to control the unrestricted development that was occurring throughout Ontario.

The legislation is now contained in s. 49 of the Planning Act, 1983, S.O. 1983, c. 1, and the control procedure is substantially the same as under s. 29.

SUBDIVISION CONTROL

Its objective was to control and regulate division of land into building lots. In the beginning it applied only to areas designated as areas of "subdivision control". However, as the cities flowed into the suburbs it became necessary to extend control to all of the province, and the act was amended accordingly on June 27, 1970 (S.O. 1970, c. 72).

S. 49(3) of the Planning Act, 1983 provides that no person shall convey, mortgage, or enter into an agreement of purchase and sale that has the effect of granting the use of or right in land for 21 years or more unless the land is:

1. within a registered plan of subdivision (s. 49(3)(a));
2. the grantor does not retain ownership in any abutting land, other than the whole of a lot on a plan of subdivision (s. 49(3)(b));
3. acquired or disposed of by the federal or provincial government, Ontario Hydro or a municipality (s. 49(3)(c));
4. acquired for construction of a transmission line as defined in the Ontario Energy Board Act, R.S.O. 1980, c. 332 (s. 49(3)(d));
5. acquired for flood and erosion control purposes, bank stabilization, shoreline management works, or preservation of environmentally sensitive lands by the Minister of Natural Resources project under s. 24 of the Conservation Authorities Act, R.S.O. 1980, c. 85 (ss. 49(3)(e), (5)(d));
6. a consent is given to convey, charge or enter an agreement (s. 49(3)(f)).

CONSENT

A consent is defined as an authorization to sever a parcel of land in order to sell, mortgage, or lease it for 21 years or more. Prior to May 3, 1965 they were granted by the Planning Board, and at that time authority was transferred to Committees of Adjustment, Land Division Committees, or where organized governments were not established, the Minister of Municipal Affairs was authorized to act (S.O. 1964, c. 90).

Where an application is found to be in the public's interest, approval is granted and a certificate is issued. It is stamped on the document or attached thereto. The document should be registered within two years after the date of the certificate, or whatever time period is provided; otherwise it lapses (s. 52(22)). Conditional consents may be obtained. The applicant has one year to perform; otherwise it lapses also.

The date and approving party should be recorded on a search of title. The result of contravention is far-reaching — no interest is created or conveyed. The onus is on the title searcher to record errors or omissions for the solicitor to review. Copies should be made of any documents you are in doubt about.

A consent is required for the following transactions:

1. transfer/deed, charge/mortgage, agreement of purchase and sale, grant, assignment or exercise of power of appointment;
2. an agreement having the effect of granting the use in land directly or by entitlement to renewal for 21 years or more, *i.e.*, a lease;
3. partial discharge of charge/mortgage (s. 49(16), (17));
4. foreclosure or exercise of power of sale (s. 49(18));
5. release or conveyance of interest by a joint tenant or tenant in common to one or more other joint tenant or tenants in common while holding abutting land (s. 49(19));
6. order under the Partition Act, R.S.O. 1980, c. 369, to partition a parcel among co-owners (s. 49(20)).

A consent is *not* required for the following transactions:

1. a quit claim deed that is not an actual conveyance;
2. dealings with condominium units and common elements under s. 50(1) of the Condominium Act, R.S.O. 1980, c. 84;
3. land acquired for transmission lines as defined in the Ontario Energy Board Act (ss. 49(3)(d), 5(c));
4. land acquired or disposed of by a federal, provincial or municipal government or Ontario Hydro (ss. 49(3)(c), (5)(b));
5. land acquired for flood and erosion control, bank stabilization, shoreline management or preservation of environmentally sensitive land by the Minister of Natural Resources, under s. 24 of the Conservation Authorities Act (ss. 49(3)(e), (5)(d));

6. an agreement having the effect of granting the use of or right in a part of a building for any period of years (s. 49(9));
7. purchaser giving back a charge/mortgage to a vendor for the consideration, provided the charge/mortgage applies to all the land described in the conveyance (s. 49(8));
8. land abutting on a horizontal plane only, *i.e.*, mineral lands (s. 49(2));
9. an agreement under s. 2 of the Drainage Act, R.S.O. 1980, c. 126 (s. 49(10));
10. a conveyance or lease by the Agricultural Rehabilitation and Development Directorate of Ontario, provided the land was acquired under one deed or transfer (s. 49(11)).

ABUTTING LANDS

Abutting lands have not been defined, but it is certain that two parcels must have a common boundary. From that viewpoint, two parcels which touch on a point only are not considered abutting (ss. 49(3)(b), 5(a)). An owner may sell either parcel without applying for a consent. What is more, the following transactions are not considered to abut:

1. where a grantor holds an easement on abutting land: *Re Vasey and Tribee Investments Ltd.*, [1971] 1 O.R. 477 (H.C.);
2. mineral rights below the surface of the ground (s. 49(2));
3. a lease on an above grade floor for more than 21 years: *Cardinière Atlantic Investment and Shipping Co. S.A. v. British Economic Insurance Co. Ltd.* (1980), 1 A.C.W.S. (2d) 360 (Ont. Co. Ct.);
4. two parcels that share only a common right of way: *Starbuck v. Thibault* (1982), 23 R.P.R. 230 (Ont. Co. Ct.);
5. lands not held in identical capacities, *i.e.*, A is first mortgagee of land abutting land owned by A, consent not required to convey land A owned: *Re Redmond et al. and Rothschild*, [1971] 1 O.R. 436 (C.A.);
6. a severance resulting from the terms of a Will, even though the conveyances are of abutting land under s. 49: *Re Kilbourn and Committee of Adjustment* (1975), 8 O.R. (2d) 142 (Div. Ct.).

REGISTERED PLANS

For the purpose of the Planning Act, a registered plan of subdivision is a plan approved under s. 50, or a predecessor thereof, and registered under the Registry Act or the Land Titles Act. Subdivision control does not apply. They include the following:

1. plans registered subsequent to the introduction of the Planning Act in 1946 which were approved by the Minister or the Ontario Municipal Board;

2. plans registered prior to 1946 (a few since that time), which were Registrar's, Judge's, Municipal or Inspector's registered plans and are not compiled plans (they are no longer permitted — Regulation 780 of the Registry Act);
3. plans registered prior to 1946, by consent, of a Registrar, a Municipality, a Judge or an Inspector of Legal Offices. They created new lots — not lots compiled from existing lots. Therefore, they are registered plans under the Planning Act and part-lot control affects all registered plans.

COMPILED PLANS

Within the category of registered plans of subdivision there are registered plans which are considered not to be registered plans of subdivision for the purpose of the Planning Act. Subdivision control still applies, but part-lot control does not, and they cannot be deemed, unless part of the plan was an earlier registered plan. Compiled plans fall into this category.

Their purpose has been to clearly identify boundaries of existing parcels previously described by metes and bounds. They are classified according to the party who ordered their registration and include the following:

1. Judge's Compiled Plan — Judge's order (discontinued January 1, 1980);
2. Municipal Compiled Plan — Assessment Office order;
3. Registrar's Compiled Plan — Land Registrar's order to clarify Registry Office records.

On registration each plan is assigned a registered plan number and the parcels lot numbers. However, because of a 1966 decision of the Court of Appeal, *Elrick v. Town of Hespeler*, [1967] 2 O.R. 448, all compiled plans are considered not to be registered plans of subdivision for the purpose of the Planning Act.

To assist title searchers in identifying these plans the Registry Act provides that a "caution" be noted on all compiled plans that "This plan is NOT a plan of subdivision within the meaning of s. 29, 32 and 33 of the Planning Act". Also, the Land Registrar is required to make an entry in the abstract book that "S. 29 of the Planning Act may continue to apply as though this plan had not been registered."

DEEMING BY-LAWS

Municipalities are empowered to pass by-laws deeming registered plans of subdivision, or part thereof, which have been registered for eight years or more *not* to be registered plans of subdivision for purposes of ss. (3), (s. 49(4)). (Refer to REGISTERED PLANS, *supra*, for what constitutes a registered plan of subdivision.)

Reasons for deeming vary from conflict over a planning program, inadequate services to design and lot sizes not conforming with current planning. What you should be aware of is that the owner of the plan must apply for a consent to sell the lots, or part thereof, and may be required to obtain approval for a new plan. Also, abutting land owners must apply for consent to sell.

The by-law is effective only upon a certified copy or a duplicate being registered in the land registration office (s. 49(23), (24)).

Finally, the by-law may be repealed on evidence of a solution to the problem. Deeming is considered to merely stop the sale of lots, so when a by-law is repealed the status of the plan as a registered plan of subdivision is not changed.

PART-LOT CONTROL BY-LAW

Part-lot control was introduced in designated areas by municipalities passing by-laws to provide control of division of lots and blocks within a plan of subdivision (a plan approved in accord with s. 29 of the Planning Act). On June 27, 1970 legislators provided province-wide control for division of lots and blocks while retaining abutting land, unless of course the abutting land is the whole of a lot or block within one or more registered plans of subdivision, or a consent to a conveyance has been obtained (s. 49(5)).

Chart 1

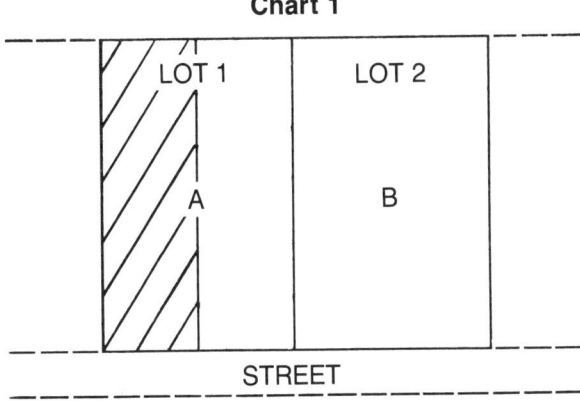

Chart 1 — Sale of part of A's property, lot 1, is subject to part-lot control; consent is required since abutting land is retained — the other half of the lot.

Chart 2

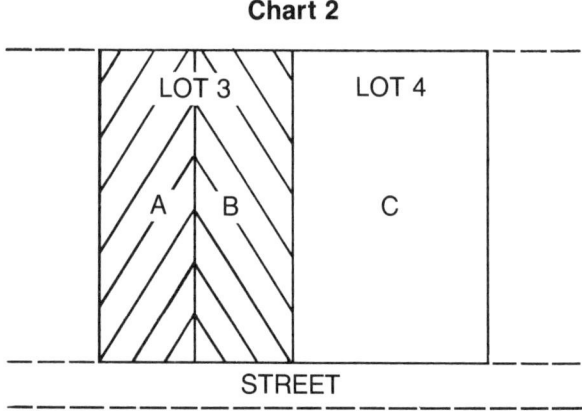

Chart 2 — If either A or B wishes to sell his entire holdings (parts lot 3), consent is not required, even though they own parts of lots, since they will not retain abutting land. C may sell all lot 4 without approval since it is a whole lot on a registered plan of subdivision.

BY-LAW REMOVING PART-LOT CONTROL

A part-lot control by-law may be removed from a plan of subdivision by the municipality registering a removing part-lot control by-law, if it is a plan approved in accordance with s. 33 of the Planning Act, or a registered plan approved prior to 1946 that is not a Registrar's, Judge's or Municipal compiled plan.

Its chief function is to facilitate transactions where obtaining an approval would be awkward or expensive. On completion of the transaction it is expedient to register a repealing by-law, to vacate the by-law removing part-lot control against all the lots and blocks dealt with. Subsequent transactions may then be carried out by the consent procedure (s. 49(7)).

Chart 3

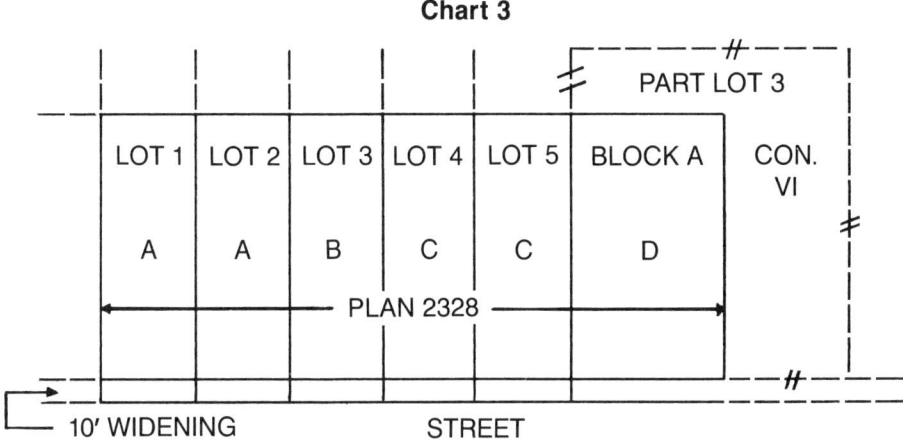

Chart 3 — Where a 10-foot strip is expropriated from the lots and blocks on plan 2328 by the municipality for road widening, each lot and block becomes part of a lot and block, and subject to part-lot control.

B can sell the remaining part of lot 3 without approval since abutting land is not retained. D can sell all or part of block A, after part-lot control is removed from Block A, even though D owns abutting land (part lot 3, concession VI) because block A is part of the registered plan of subdivision.

A by-law removing part-lot control could be registered against lots 1, 2, 4 and 5 to allow sales without the required consent. Since lot 3 has been sold, it need not be removed from it.

SIGNIFICANT DATES

Dates relating to amendments enacted under the Planning Act throughout the last few years which are important to a title searcher include:

1. June 15, 1967 — the Planning Amendment Act, 1967, S.O. 1967, c. 75, provided that contravention of s. 29 or its predecessors prior to this date was forgiven;
2. May 2, 1968 — the effective date for repeal of the 10-acre exemption (S.O. 1968, c. 96);
3. June 27, 1970 — the effective date for universal subdivision control and part-lot control throughout Ontario; prior to this date subdivision control was designated in certain areas by municipal by-law registered on title; a part-lot control by-law was also registered where necessary to sever a lot on a plan of subdivision;

4. December 15, 1978 — the effective date for forgiveness of contravention prior to registration of a plan of subdivision, registration of a description under the Condominium Act or a conveyance with a consent under the Planning Act (retroactive effect) (s. 49(14));
5. March 31, 1979 — the legislation provided that where a parcel of land was created by a conveyance with a consent, Planning Act consent was not applicable to subsequent conveyances for the identical parcel, even though the grantor owned abutting land; assuming that this amendment is not retroactive, this will only affect conveyances after this date (s. 49(12));
6. August 1, 1983 — the effective date for s. 49(6), the remaining part of a parcel can be conveyed prior to the part or parts which have been the subject of a consent, provided the consent has not lapsed.

L.R.R.A., 1984 STATEMENTS

On a final note, the LRRA introduced aggressive changes to subdivision control on November 1, 1984 that reduced the time and the aggravation often associated with title searching. The changes legislated are contained in s. 49(21a) to (21d) of the Planning Act, 1983. Section 49(21a) provides that where the statements, replacing the former affidavits, contained in Boxes 13 and 14 of the new transfer/deed, Form 1 are signed by the transferor, the transferor's solicitor and the transferee's solicitor, contravention of s. 49, or a predecessor thereof, does not and shall be deemed never to have had the effect of preventing the conveyance or any interest in the land. In other words, all contraventions of s. 49, past and present, are forgiven, and searches for prior compliance are eliminated.

However, the statement's effectiveness depends on the co-operation of the solicitors. Solicitors acting for the transferor have been known to disagree as to its merits and refuse to sign; signing is entirely voluntary. Reference should be made on your search of title as to whether or not the document was signed by all three.

The penalty for anyone who knowingly makes a false statement is major (s. 49(21a)).

CHAPTER 10

EASEMENTS AND RIGHTS OF WAY

Easements and rights of way are a right or interest in someone else's property.

Once an easement has been validly created it is conveyed whether specifically referred to in subsequent deeds and transfers or not. It runs with the land when the dominant tenement (the land benefiting by the easement) is sold. The purchaser gets the rights that the vendor had, and when the servient tenement (the land over or through which the easement runs) is sold, the purchaser is subject to the rights of the easement. If one person buys both tenements the easement merges.

The lands to be benefited by an easement are set out in the document creating it, and the Land Registrar abstracts the benefit of the easement on the dominant and servient land. In some cases prior encumbrances are also entered.

Under the Registry system it is the title searcher's duty to record the following particulars:

(a) the width of the easement;
(b) the term of the reservation or if it is in perpetuity;
(c) restrictions re: building on it;
(d) covenants to repair, restore, *etc.,* the surface;
(e) Planning Act affidavit stating that the conveyance complies with s. 49. They are usually in perpetuity and affect part of the lot so compliance is required;
(f) execution and affidavits where necessary;
(g) compare subsequent descriptions.

Under the Land Titles system it is necessary to establish (a) to (d) only, as outlined above.

Easements and rights of way can only be lost by abandonment or be released by a grant or transfer.

Part of the preparation in creating a grant or transfer of right of way is searching the land of the servient tenement to establish who owns it and if he has the right to grant such right of way.

Prior to registering a transfer of easement under the Land Titles system, a search for writs of executions should be made. The transfer will be entered on the register subject to any that are outstanding.

Section 23 of the Registry Act provides that an old easement description such as " a right of way over a laneway now in existence and leading to the road allowance between lots 5 and 6" is no longer acceptable. A reference plan, or a metes and bounds description, which complies with the regulations should be submitted on registration.

A specific grant of an easement is where A owns a parcel of land and grants B a right of way across it in perpetuity, for passage and repassage of persons, vehicles and animals, over and along a 10-foot strip, *etc.*

A right of way may also be established by reservation — reserving unto the grantor, his heirs and assigns, a right of way, for passage and repassage of persons, vehicles and animals over . . . , *etc.*

An implied grant of easement is created when an owner of a parcel of land fronting on a highway sells the rear half without providing the purchaser access to the highway. The law may imply a right of way of necessity.

In reverse, if the owner sells the front half without reserving a right of way to give himself access to the highway, the parcel will be landlocked. As you may guess, these are uncommon occurrences.

EASEMENTS IN COMMON USE

Mutual Drives

A mutual drive is a strip of land shared by adjoining neighbours. They are not unusual in the older parts of cities and are described as follows: The whole of lot 16 according to Plan 2345; together with a right of way over the northerly four feet of the lands lying immediately to the south of the lands described herein. And subject to a right of way over the southerly four feet of the lands described herein.

Party Wall Agreements

Party wall agreements are also common in the older sections of cities. Houses were built right on the property line. The strip cannot be sold and is known as a right of way of mutual support. Reference is made to it in the description.

Easements of Necessity

Cottage properties often require access over farm lands to get to a highway or a right of way over the rear of all the neighbours' cottage lands along a beach. In the latter case, a search must be made over each individual parcel for evidence of ownership and the right to grant the right of way.

Public Utility Easements

Bell Canada and the local hydro commission have an easement usually over the rear four feet of each lot in new subdivisions. This land cannot be built on since it is for service lines. The land is described as parts of Lot 25 according to Plan M-1392 registered in the Land Registry Office for the Land Titles Division of Toronto and York South, designated as PARTS 3 and 4 on Reference Plan 66R-2312 deposited in the said office, subject to an easement in favour of Bell Canada over the said PART 4 on Reference Plan 66R-2312 for the purposes as set out in instrument number A-32563.

Transfers of easements to Bell Canada, a privately owned company, require Planning Act consent. The Planning Act, 1983 exempted Ontario Hydro from this stipulation. But prior transfers that contravened the act were not forgiven.

Underground Sewer and Water Lines

The description for an underground sewer and water line easement is usually difficult to plot and accuracy is important because it would be unfortunate if you found that a building was constructed on the easement. Of course, if you have a survey it will be indicated thereon.

Easement by Prescription

Where land is registered under the Registry system, and someone has used a neighbour's property as a short cut for 20 years without interruption, consent from the owner, or agreement in writing, he may have established a permanent easement by possession or prescription. Under the Land Titles system an easement can be established only by a grant of easement from the registered owner.

Part II

THE LAND TITLES ACT

CHAPTER 11

THE LAND TITLES ACT

The majority of the land in Ontario is registered under the Land Titles Act, R.S.O. 1980, c. 230, and amendments thereto provided for a steady increase in applications for Registry Office lands to be registered under that Act. This includes all new plans of subdivision and condominium properties.

The sustaining principle behind the Land Titles Act is that it guarantees that title under a guarantee of indemnity is vested in a certain person. In the event of error, a claim may be made to the Land Titles Assurance Fund.

The system is more sophisticated than the Registry system so title searching is less complex.

It is a register of titles and not of deeds as in the Registry system and the registered documents are evidence supporting the title. The relevant section from all documents registered subsequent to the Patent is recorded in a book referred to as the register in the order of registration.

However, since the enactment of the L.R.R.A., 1984, relevant information from documents registered against parcels of land that have been designated to the POLARIS system is stored in a computer index and retrieved on a printout at the computer terminal.

Plans of subdivision registered in this office differ, in that they are identified by a number which is prefixed by the letter "M", *e.g.*, M-2345. Recently, the procedure was changed to the same numbering system as is applied to reference plans. The number now allocated is prefixed by the number of the particular Registry Office and the letter "M", *e.g.*, 66M-2345.

A few registered plans prefixed by the letter "D" are in existence. The reference is usually allocated to lands consolidated by a municipality or to several parcels owned by a developer to facilitate future transactions with the land. There are also miscellaneous plans with the prefix "MISC" and they are plans deposited, filed or registered by the Minister of Transportation and Communications.

However, there are lots on concessions under the Land Titles system which have not been subdivided, or were subdivided prior to entry under that system and have not been resubdivided by an "M" plan (a common reference). In that case, the Registry Office abstract will disclose an entry by which the registered owner made application to register the land under the Land Titles system. The application will indicate the necessary Land Titles reference to obtain the register, *i.e.*, the parcel and section number.

PARCELS AND SECTIONS

A parcel of land may incorporate a lot, a block, a one-foot reserve, a road allowance, or a multiple thereof, or a part of a lot, or block, or reserve, or road allowance. A page is opened in the register, and a particular parcel is identified by the number and section allotted to it and recorded at the top of each page, and not by the lot and plan as under the Registry system.

The parcel and section numbers are required to obtain the register. In the past, the system for establishing these numbers had no particular significance. However, in recent years a system has been introduced to establish a consecutive numbering system for all lands that are subdivided, *e.g.*, Lot 250, Plan M-1684 would be designated parcel 250-1, Section M-1684 and subsequent transfers of the lot are allocated new parcel numbers, *i.e.*, 250-2, 250-3, *etc.* The parcel identifies with the lot number and the section with the plan number.

Not all offices have adopted this system and some still have a type of consecutive numbering system in which the parcel is given a number or a letter and a number, and the section usually identifies with the municipality, *e.g.*, Parcel S-8301 or 88863, Section Sudbury East (S.S.E.).

A parcel index is available to the public and it lists all the parcels and sections created prior to the new system. It is of value to those who have not been provided with the necessary information and is referred to frequently when searching abutting lands.

DOCUMENT REFERENCE

The reference to documents provided by the L.R.R.A., 1984 is described in Chapter 4, Registered Documents. Prior to that legislation, documents differed in form and name. A deed reference in the Land Titles system was a transfer, a mortgage was a charge, and assignment of mortgage was a transfer of charge and a discharge of mortgage was a cessation of charge.

Freehold Register

SECTION M-67   PARCEL   PLAN-1   PAGE 1

Under Application D-35 and 4998 L.T.
ONTARIO HOUSING CORPORATION, is the owner in fee simple with an *absolute Title* of:

THAT PART of LOT 19, CONCESSION 7, *in the Township of Barton,* County of Wentworth, now in the City of Hamilton, and *designated as PART 1* on a Plan of survey of record in the office of Land Titles at Hamilton, as *62R-344,* and *PART 1* on a Plan of Survey or record in the office of Land Titles at Hamilton, as 62R-344, and PART 1 on a Plan of Survey of record in said office of Land Titles as *WHR-123.*

The Title of the said owner is *subject to:*

1. The exceptions and qualifications in The Land Titles Act.
2. Instrument 167546 H.L. (Wentworth) registered on 29th June, 1961, being By-law 9375 of The Corporation of the City of Hamilton, passed June 27th, 1961, re an area of Subdivision Control.
DATED at Hamilton, this 21st day of May, 1971.
MASTER OF TITLES.

Registered in the Office of Land Titles at Hamilton, the 21st day of June, 1971, lays out part of the above Parcel into the following, namely:

1stly — Lots 1 to 70 . . . .
2ndly — STREET — Caroga Court
3rdly — 1' Reserve, Block A.

MASTER OF TITLES.

Originally and Recently Parcel 19-2
Section Bar — 7
The Province of Ontario claims no lien against this Parcel under The Corporations Tax Act or The Retail Sales Act in respect of any previous ownership.

PLAN M-67
Plan Document 5381 L.T.

INHIBITING ORDER

Complied with under 5691 L.T.

~~By Order of the Master of Titles made the 21st day of June, 1971, attached to PLAN DOCUMENT 5381 L.T. no dealings with the hereinafter described lands may be accepted for registration until the following Agreement and Transfer in favour of The Corporation of the City of Hamilton, have been registered.~~
~~DATE OF AGREEMENT AND TRANSFER~~
~~LOTS AND BLOCKS AFFECTED   February 25, 1971~~
~~All Lots and Blocks in the Plan   Agreement~~

Freehold Register

PARCEL PLAN - 1   SECTION M-67   PAGE 2

Notice

By 5691 L.T. dated and registered the 14th July, 1971, Notice is hereby entered of a Subdivision Agreement attached thereto dated the 25th February, 1971, between ONTARIO HOUSING CORPORATION and THE CORPORATION OF THE CITY OF HAMILTON.

Authorized Signing Officer.

TRANSFERS LOT 5

By Transfer 5695 L.T. dated 5th July, 1971, registered 14th July, 1971, LOT 5 on PLAN M-67 was transferred to *GEORGE C. KOVACS. Now entered as PARCEL LOT 5-1 SECTION M-67.*

TRANSFERS BLOCK A

By transfer 5791 L.T., dated 23rd July, 1971, registered 27th July, 1971, *BLOCK A on PLAN M-67 was transferred to The Corporation of the City of Hamilton. Now entered as PARCEL LOT A-1, SECTION M-67.*

Deputy Master of Titles.

TRANSFERS *PART OF LOT 6*

Under Transfer 69564 L.T. dated 12th October, 1976, registered 25th April, 1978, *THAT PART OF LOT 6 on PLAN M-67, designated as PART 1 on Reference Plan 62R-3751, was transferred to THE CORPORATION OF THE CITY OF HAMILTON. Now entered as PARCEL LOT 6-1 SECTION M-67.*
62R-3751

EASEMENT
Part 2 on Plan 62R-3751

By Transfer — 71405 L.T. dated 1st May, 1978, registered 16th June, 1978, ONTARIO HOUSING CORPORATION hereby grants to THE CORPORATION OF THE CITY OF HAMILTON the right, licence, liberty, privilege and easement or right in the nature of an easement on, over, under and through the land hereinafter described namely: as those *Parts of LOTS 7 AND 8 on PLAN M-67 described as PART 2 on Reference Plan 62R-3751* for itself and others under its direction, to construct, landscape, maintain and replace a berm as a sound barrier, in, over, along and upon the above lands and do such incidental work as may be necessary. The Transferor covenants that the said lands will be kept clear of all obstructions as may be necessary for the use of the easement. The Transferee covenants to be responsible for any damage caused by the negligence of the Transferee and others under its direction in the course of exercising the rights hereby transferred.

Authorized Signing Officer.

THE TITLE SEARCH

Searching titles under the Land Titles system is relatively simple as compared to the Registry system. The distinguishing feature about it is that the current parcel shows the present registered owner and that he or she has an absolute title, subject to charges, agreements, easements, or by-laws that are noted on the register. Particulars of the description are noted. Each parcel is subject to the exceptions and qualifications of the Land Titles Act.

All prior defects in title are cleared when the land is transferred from the Registry system to the Land Titles system under a procedure referred to as First Application. Only outstanding encumbrances are reflected on the parcel register at that time.

As in the Registry system, there is a fee for each parcel in the register, plan or document which is examined. Forms for requisitioning parcels, plans and documents are provided by the Land Registrar and if they are completed in detail, much time may be saved when they are presented at the counter.

It is customary to order a copy of the register. However, if you wish to study it and make notes from it, you may do so. Then proceed as follows:

1. Order a white print of the plan of subdivision and:
   (a) verify the size of the lot as recorded in the offer to purchase, or the survey with the measurements shown on the plan, and
   (b) verify dedication of one-foot reserves and road widenings.
2. Establish the parcel and section numbers for all abutting lands, either by identifying them with the lot and plan numbers, e.g., lot 41, Plan M-234 would be parcel 41-1, Plan M-234, or from the index provided for that purpose. Check abutting lands (see Chapter 3 under "Abutting Land Searches" and Chapter 9, The Planning Act for dates to search from) and note on your search whether or not the registered owner of the subject lands owned any of the abutting lands within the prescribed time.
3. Get particulars of outstanding documents such as charges and agreements shown on the current parcel, or referred to on a prior parcel. (Refer to Chapter 4, Registered Documents.)
4. Check for the Land Titles signing officer's signature on the register after each document.
5. Order copies of all reference plans that affect the subject lands.
6. A day sheet for current registrations should be requested from the counter staff, if the office has not adopted the practice of pencilling them on the register at the time of registration.
7. Obtain an execution certificate against the registered owner(s).
8. Check the highways and Trans-Canada Pipe Line registers (the

entries are not made on freehold registers, yet you are deemed to have notice).

A typical parcel register, as set up in the register, is shown on pages 93-94.

PROCEDURE SUBSEQUENT TO FIRST APPLICATION

Where land is transferred from the Registry system to the Land Titles system the owner of the land makes an application to do so. On acceptance of the land the following procedure is initiated.

1. Where land is on a lot on a concession, a register is allotted for the particular municipality, *e.g.*, Etobicoke, until further dealings with the land commence.
2. A parcel and section number is designated and recorded at the top of the page, *e.g.*, Parcel E-1, Section Etobicoke. The application number, the registered owner, the land description and particulars of encumbrances, *etc.*, that the land is subject to, follow in that order. However, the Registry Office reference (Plan 3456, Borough of Etobicoke) for land subdivided prior to first application is incorporated in the land title reference, *i.e.*, Parcel-Plan 3456, Section Etob.
3. The register is signed by the Land Registrar or one of his deputies certifying that, *e.g.*, John Smith is the owner with an absolute title, subject to the encumbrances, *etc.*
4. A plan of subdivision is usually registered immediately after the registration of the owner's application and, in that event, what is referred to as a "parcel plan" is set up and designated parcel plan 1. The section is allotted the registration number of the plan, M-678. An inhibiting order, whereby the owner is obligated to comply with certain responsibilities, is registered by the municipality and is a part of the plan document. Reference to prior parcels and sections and to corporate owners is made in the margin.
5. When all the lots, blocks and reserves are sold and transferred to new parcels, the parcel plan is closed.
    Several lots are often transferred to one person, usually a builder. They are re-entered in parcel plan 2, Section M-678. Individual lots as sold are re-entered in separate parcels; *e.g.*, lot 24 would be designated parcel 24-1. When parts of that lot are sold, *e.g.*, the west half, a reference plan is deposited on title showing the PART to be transferred and it is re-entered as parcel 24-2.
6. Between the date of registration and the entry of a document on the register a few days may elapse so a temporary note of the registration number only is made in pencil on the register in most

offices; in others it is recorded on a day sheet. The document is available for inspection in the meantime. Even after it is recorded in full in the register it is not considered registered until an authorized signing officer, A.S.O., signs the entry.

7. A note is made in the margin, opposite the transfer, "Lots 90-100 transferred." Thus one can tell at a glance what lots have been transferred and severed from the original parcel.

8. The new parcel is set out in the register, on the next page, the parcel, Parcel 90-100-1, and section, Section M-678, recorded at the top of the page.

9. The prior parcel number is recorded at the top of the left corner of the page, *e.g.*, originally Parcel E-1, Section Etob. This is only for identification of prior parcels.

10. The new parcel is identical to the original parcel in that the owner, encumbrances and description are recorded.

11. The names of the prior owners are ruled off parcel Plan 1 when all the lots are severed, except where the transfer is subject to an easement, conditions, *etc.*

12. Where cessations of charges, compliance with agreements and inhibiting orders, releases of cautions and discharges of construction liens and their certificates of action are registered, the registration number, date and signing officer's signature are noted in the margin opposite the entry for such charge, *etc.* The particulars, parties, *etc.*, are not recorded in a separate entry as in the case of other registrations. Such charge, *etc.*, is then ruled off and of no further interest.

13. Where a caution is superseded by a transfer, that notation is made in the margin with the registration number of the transfer, date and the signing officer's signature.

FREEHOLD PARCEL REGISTER

The legal description for the freehold land in each parcel is entered at the top of the first page of the parcel register, *e.g.*, all of Lots 2 and 3 and part of Block A on Plan M-340 (City of Brampton) registered in the Land Titles Office for the Land Titles Division of Peel (No. 43) at Brampton, designated PART 1, 2 and 3 on a plan of survey of record in the said office as Plan 43R-8278. Subject to a right of way in favour of the Corporation of The City of Brampton to enter upon that part of the said Block A on Plan M-340, designated as PART 2 on the said Plan 43R-8278.

Descriptions in subsequent transfers, charges or leases for the whole or part of the above-mentioned land are as follows:

1. the whole of the parcel—(Lots 2 and 3 and part of Block A), a very simple description may be used, "the whole of the parcel";
2. part of the parcel—(part of Block A), the document should contain the parcel register description;
3. the remainder of the parcel—(Lots 2 and 3), "the remainder of the parcel" is all that is required.

LEASEHOLD PARCEL REGISTER

Registration entries for a freehold parcel of land on which a developer proposes to construct a large office building are transferred to a lease-hold register on the owner of the land providing the developer with a 99-year ground lease.

Leasehold parcels are set up in the same manner as freehold, except that leasehold is noted on the register at the top of each page. An entry is made on the freehold parcel, "Entered in leasehold parcel 112-1, Section M-893 under Lease #A-3468." The original parcel and recent parcel number, *i.e.*, the parcel that the leasehold parcel came from, are noted in the upper left hand corner.

Ontario Housing Corporation, Ontario Land Corporation or the Crown under the Mining Act or the Public Lands Act often hold the leasehold estate also.

LEASEHOLD MERGE

Where the lessee acquires the freehold estate, the leasehold estate merges in the freehold and it becomes subject to any interest to which the leasehold estate was subject prior to the merging and in the same ranking as to priorities. Note the abstracting procedure that follows:

1. A new parcel is opened to combine the freehold and leasehold estates. Prior encumbrances affecting both estates are entered in order of registration followed by the Transfer.
2. The Transfer is entered on the previous freehold parcel with a notation, "together with the leasehold estate in the said land lease number _____ having merged under the said transfer."
3. The prior leasehold parcel is closed out with a notation, "re-entry, the above parcel and lease having merged under transfer number _____ and entered as parcel _____ ."

MINERAL LANDS PARCEL REGISTER

The land in Northern Ontario is usually registered under the Land Titles Act. Frequently, the surface rights of such lands are severed from the mining rights and all ores, mines and minerals on or under the lands are conveyed with the mining rights land.

When surface rights only are transferred, a new parcel is opened in the Land Titles Office. The mining rights remain vested in the owner and a notation is made on the original parcel to indicate that it now contains mining rights only.

There are likely to be numerous easements registered on the surface rights lands for mining rights, since right of access for mining is reserved to the vested owner. The agreement of purchase and sale should make reference to exactly what rights are to be sold. Consent to sever such rights pursuant to s. 49 of the Planning Act is not required because they are lands that abut on a horizontal plane (s. 49.2).

Withdrawal of Land from Land Titles System

Since this system is so much simpler than the Registry system it does seem strange to see an application of withdrawal on title. This happens when an owner of several parcels registered under the Registry system wishes to register them in one office to facilitate future transactions. The application must contain a description suitable to both systems.

APPLICATION TO CONSOLIDATE PARCELS

Where a registered owner owns more than one parcel under the Land Titles system, not necessarily adjoining land, he may make application to consolidate them in one parcel. The previous description may be retained, except where a part of a parcel is being consolidated; then a reference plan is usually required for the part.

CAUTIONS

Under the Registry Act anyone may register a claim, or agreement against property, while under the Land Titles Act a person who claims to have an interest in land or in a charge of which he is not the registered owner may register a caution to protect that interest. The registered owner of the land or charge cannot deal with the land or charge without the consent of the cautioner. Ss. 129 (4) and (5) of the Land Titles Act provide that as of January 1, 1980 a caution will automatically expire five years from the date of its registration unless it is renewed. When it ceases to have effect the Land Registry may delete the entry from the register.

Certificate of Ownership of Land and of Charge

The Land Titles Amendment Act, 1979 provided that Certificates of Ownership and Certificates of Ownership of Charge would no longer be issued. Outstanding certificates must be surrendered prior to registration of new transfers or charges.

REGISTERS

Ontario Reg. 75/82 under the Land Titles Act, R.S.O. 1980, c. 230, which replaced Regulation 552, came into force on May 1, 1982. Each Land Registry Office for every land titles division must provide registers, similar to the parcel register, referred to as:

1. A "highways register" under s. 43(1) and (2) as referred to in s. 75(2) of the Act, for recording plans deposited, filed or registered by the Minister of Transportation and Communications under the Public Transportation and Highway Improvement Act, R.S.O. 1980, c. 421. The registration number allocated to such plans is prefixed by "MISC.", for miscellaneous, *e.g.*, MISC. 345. Note that the Land Registrar enters documents registered for highway lands on that register only; they are not repeated in the freehold register. Yet you are deemed to have notice, so suffice to say, search both.

2. A "Trans-Canada Pipe Line register" under s. 44, as referred to in s. 75(3) of the Act, shall be kept in every registry office through which a pipe line constructed or owned by TransCanada PipeLines Limited passes. "MISC." again prefixes the plan number allocated. Note again that the Land Registrar makes entries on this register only, even though the documents may affect freehold land. You are deemed to have notice, so examine both registers.

3. A "fee and receiving book" under s. 45(1) and as referred to in s. 75(1) of the Act is provided for the entry of every document received for registration. On completion of the entry of a document in the parcel register, leasehold register or condominium register, a notation of the completion shall be entered opposite the entry of the document in the fee and receiving book.

   When registration of a document has been delayed, a re-entry is made in the suspense book. On registration of all the documents on a page, or re-entry in the suspense book, and where preceding pages have been ruled out, the Land Registrar rules the page with a diagonal line to indicate that the documents entered thereon, and on preceding pages, have been registered, rejected or entered in the suspense book.

4. A "suspense book" for all documents of which registration has been delayed. When the documents have been dealt with, the pages are dealt with in the same manner as the fee and receiving book.

5. A register for "cautions" under s. 44(1) of the Act.

6. A register for "powers of attorney".

Part III

THE CONDOMINIUM ACT

CHAPTER 12

THE CONDOMINIUM ACT

The Condominium Act, R.S.O. 1980, c. 84, governs all condominium development and ownership in Ontario. The condominium owner, whether it be residential or industrial property, holds title to a particular unit and, at the same time, shares with fellow owners the title and cost of operation of the balance of the property constituting the condominium. It is a distinct type of property ownership rather than a distinct style of building.

The declaration contains a description of the units and allocation of ownership of the common elements and common expenses. Rules for operating the corporation are incorporated in the by-laws, and the rules relating to all the property, except the units, are embodied in the common element document.

Since September 1, 1967, in counties or districts where a Land Titles Office is maintained, the declaration and description should be registered under the Land Titles Act, R.S.O. 1980, c. 230. Where land is registered under a registry division the title of the declarant should be certified under the Certification of Titles Act, R.S.O. 1980, c. 61, showing the declarant to be the owner in fee simple.

A condominium, without share capital, whose members are the owners is established on registration of the declaration and description. It is given a name which identifies with the land registry division and it is numbered in numerical sequence, *e.g.*, Cochrane Condominium no. 678.

CONDOMINIUM REGISTER

The condominium register is deemed to be a register index or an abstract index, depending on which system the lands are registered under. Four registers are set up and a title searcher should get copies of or make notes from all four.

After registration of the declaration and description, if the land is registered under the Land Titles Act the Land Registrar carries out the following:

1. Enters the registration particulars for the declaration and description in the existing parcel register. Where the condominium lands comprise the whole of that parcel, a closing entry is made on the parcel.
2. Opens a new register under the Condominium Act and re-enters the land on the *Property Parcel Register*. All the documents affecting the land and the declaration and description are entered in order of their registration.
3. Arranges the *Constitutional Index* and enters the declaration, description and by-laws.
4. Arrranges the *Common Elements and General Index* and enters the declaration and description. Full details of easements and rights of way are not recorded since there is not a conventional description for this parcel.
5. Arranges a *Unit Register*. The units and levels are recorded in numerical sequence, similar to that of the land titles parcel page. To conduct a search, it is necessary to have the name and number of the condominium corporation and the number assigned to each unit and level.

Outstanding charges, agreements, liens, easements, *etc.*, are not carried forward to the final register. Subsequently registered documents only are entered, so all four registers must be checked. Partial discharges (for units) for blanket mortgages recorded on the Common Elements and General Index and the Property Parcel Register are entered on the unit register.

Indoor parking space provided in a condominium building is usually assigned to a unit. However, some buildings divided such space into units which are purchased. In that case, a search of the particular parking space unit is also required. The offer to purchase should disclose the particulars necessary to search. Plans of survey are available, showing a detailed description of all the units.

Where a condominium is registered under the Registry Act, the Land Registrar proceeds as follows:

1. Enters the declaration and description in the existing abstract book for the condominium property.
2. Opens an abstract index for the condominium property and abstracts the following:
    (i) Certificate of Title as registered under the Certification of Titles Act. (It is registered prior to the condominium.)
    (ii) All documents referred to in Schedule B and C of the certificate.
    (iii) The declaration, description and all intervening registered documents affecting the property.

3. Opens a Constitution Index and abstracts the declaration and description.
4. Opens the Common Elements and General Index and records the declaration and description.
5. Opens a Unit Index, *i.e.*, a page for each unit of each level of the condominium property.

Of course, the function of the Condominium Register is irrelevant once the condominium property is registered under the L.R.R.A., 1984, but it is still maintained for public reference.

A printout of title may be obtained at the computer terminal and the PIN necessary for access is listed in the Terminal PIN Index. The printout lists the registered owner and outstanding encumbrances. Currently, the blanket charge/mortgage and construction liens entered on the Common Elements and General Index are provided on the unit printout.

Executions should be searched against the condominium corporation as well as the vendor-developer.

Liens against corporate owners are now registered on title.

As mentioned in Chapter 9, The Planning Act, abutting unit owner searches are not required.

The owners of each of the units must contribute to the common expenses of the condominium corporation. Failure to do so creates a lien against the particular unit. The Act provides that the Condominium Board has three months from the date of default to register a notice of the lien; otherwise it ceases to exist.

The solicitor for the purchaser should obtain an estoppel certificate from the corporation which sets out particulars of default to the date of closing. If it is not given within seven days following a request for it, the Act deems a Certificate to have been given stating that default has not occurred.

Part IV

CLOSINGS

CHAPTER 13

CLOSING THE TRANSACTION

Considerable time usually lapses from the completion of the search until the closing date of the transaction. The solicitor, who may be acting for a purchaser, a vendor or a chargee/mortgagee sends a representative (student or title searcher) to the land registration office to exchange documents with the solicitor acting on the other side of the transaction and to conduct the necessary registrations.

SUBSEARCHES

Under the Registry Act you are required to obtain the abstract book, bring the search up to date and, if documents were registered subsequent to the completion date of the search, advise your solicitor. Also check the following:

1. the day book, also known as the fee book, is a concise recording of the entries which the Registry Office clerks did not have time to enter in the abstract book, *e.g.*, "#26432, registered 12 January, 1979 — Lot 16, Plan 3412, ETOBICOKE." This takes considerable time on busy days.
2. documents which the clerks did not have time to enter in the day book;
3. documents held by people in the registration line ahead of the person closing the transaction which should be checked but usually are not. This practice should not be overlooked if you have reason to believe that a lien might be registered that day.

Under the Land Titles Act a subsearch is less complicated. When a document is presented at the registration counter, a subsearch of the parcel register is made at that time. The document will not be accepted by the registration clerk if the parcel register indicates the vendor or chargor named in your document is not identical to the owner indicated on the register.

Under the L.R.R.A., 1984 a property is subsearched on tendering a document for registration. The name of the transferor or chargor on the document must coincide with the owner indicated on the terminal screen. If there are documents the staff did not have time to load into the computer, the clerks will permit you to review them.

EXECUTIONS

Where land is registered in the Registry Office and executions were not searched at the time of searching the title against all previous owners, then do so now and hope for the best. Otherwise, search against the vendor only. Particulars of outstanding executions are usually obtained at the Sheriff's Office. In Toronto, the office is on the Fourth Floor of the Registry Office building.

A certificate is required against the vendor under the Land Titles system, and on a condominium purchase it is required for the condominium corporation as well as the vendor.

CHATTEL SEARCHES

When the purchaser is also purchasing chattel property (stoves, drapes, *etc.*) of any value a chattel search should be conducted against the vendor just in case someone else claims an interest. The offices for searching are usually in the Registry Office. In Toronto it is located at 393 University Avenue, Third Floor.

ALTERATIONS TO DOCUMENTS

Unfortunately, a great many of the documents presented for registration have errors in description of the lands, or of the parties. If they are checked prior to proceeding to the registration counter a good deal of time may be saved. The person who executes a document must initial alterations thereto. Likewise, there should be no alterations to the Affidavit of Residence and of Value of the Consideration which has already been sworn.

The Land Registrar or counter staff must have actual knowledge that an alteration was made without the proper authority before he can reject a document presented for registration.

CLOSING WHEN ACTING FOR THE PURCHASER

Obtain the following from the vendor's solicitor or his representative:

1. deed/transfer in duplicate, fully executed with the Affidavit of Residence and of Value of the Consideration. Check corporate seal

closely if affixed; its use is now optional. However, if it is not used the L.R.R.A., 1984 has provided that a statement must be completed by the officers that they have the authority to bind the company;

2. a copy of the insurance policy and transfer if it is transferable; check the amounts and dates with the statement of adjustments;
3. a copy of charge/mortgage statements, and the charge/mortgage to be assumed. They should be in accordance with the statement of adjustments and the agreement of purchase and sale;
4. addresses for charge/mortgage payments;
5. where a discharge of a charge/mortgage is not available, get a charge/mortgage statement showing balance owing, with funds payable to the chargee/mortgagee; also get an undertaking to obtain and register the discharge and provide registration particulars;
6. vendor's undertaking to readjust taxes, public utilities, insurance premiums and amounts outstanding on charges/mortgages to date of closing;
7. tax bill in accordance with the statement of adjustments;
8. direction re: funds and charge/mortgage back where chargee/mortgagee is not the vendor;
9. old title documents;
10. keys;
11. leases and assignment of leases or acknowledgements by tenants and directions to tenants to pay future rents to the purchaser, where applicable;
12. warranty re: urea formaldehyde foam insulation;
13. declaration re: s. 116 of the Income Tax Act of Canada — not non-resident;
14. bill of sale re: chattel ownership.

The purchaser's solicitor registers the deed and transcribes the address of the grantee or any person claiming an interest on the back thereof, pays the prescribed registration fee and the land transfer tax.

ACTING FOR THE VENDOR

The vendor's solicitor receives the following from the purchaser's solicitor:

1. charge/mortgage back, where applicable, in accordance with the statement of adjustments and the agreement of purchase and sale;
2. certified cheque payable to and in the amount set out in the statement of adjustments, or payable to, as set out in a direction signed by the vendor;
3. a direction from the purchaser's solicitor authorizing the vendor's

solicitor to describe the purchasers in the deed according to his instructions rather than according to the offer to purchase;

4. evidence of insurance in amount of charge/mortgage showing the vendor as first or second chargee/mortgagee.

The vendor's solicitor registers the charge/mortgage back when applicable, and remains with the purchaser's solicitor until the deed or transfer is accepted by the Land Registrar.

ACTING FOR THE CHARGEE/MORTGAGEE

The purchaser's solicitor gives the following:

1. copy of the statement of adjustments;
2. tax certificate or a receipted tax bill;
3. charge/mortgage in duplicate;
4. copy of charge/mortgage statement for an existing prior mortgage;
5. post-dated cheques, if necessary;
6. a copy of the insurance policy and the transfer indicating the new chargee/mortgagee's name thereon;
7. evidence of discharges of charges/mortgages or encumbrances to be discharged on or before closing in accordance with the agreement of purchase and sale.

The purchaser's solicitor receives:

1. a certified cheque for the proceeds of the charge/mortgage;
2. address to which mortgage payments are to be made;
3. direction re: mortgage payments if necessary.

CLOSING A CONDOMINIUM PURCHASE

Solicitor for the purchaser receives the following from the solicitor for the vendor:

1. transfer;
2. occupancy agreement if the condominium has not been registered prior to closing;
3. estoppel certificate;
4. keys;
5. tax certificate;
6. insurance.

UNDERTAKINGS

It is often necessary for solicitors to close transactions prior to completing all the details, and under such circumstances undertakings are necessary.

They should not be given indiscriminately and a student should give them only under his principal's instruction. Solicitors often have those that are necessary prepared prior to closing.

They fall into two categories:

1. a personal undertaking — this creates a personal liability on the solicitor, and
2. a client's undertaking — it follows that the client should sign; however, in the client's absence the solicitor may undertake on his or her behalf with no personal liability.

The most frequent undertakings are to obtain and register discharges of charges/mortgages, simply because insurance companies, trust companies and banks will not prepare a discharge until they have received the money. One should not be given where an individual is a chargee/mortgagee.

An undertaking, direction, *etc.*, should be prepared in duplicate and read as follows:

Personal

From:
To:

Re:

In consideration of closing the above transaction I hereby personally undertake to obtain and register a discharge of charge/mortgage No. 3245, held by The Royal Bank of Canada within two months, and notify you of registration particulars.

On Behalf Of Client

To:

And To: Barrister and Solicitor

Re: sale to

UNDERTAKING

In consideration of, and notwithstanding the closing of the above-noted transaction, the undersigned Vendors hereby undertake as follows:

1. To pay all public utility rates to date of closing, including hydro, gas (if applicable) and water rates;
2. To re-adjust any items on the Statement of Adjustments, upon written demand, if necessary;

3. To pay or re-adjust all realty taxes to date of closing;
4. To pay all insurance premiums to date of closing and to take steps necessary to effectively transfer the policy to the Purchaser;
5. To fill the fuel tank in accordance with the Statement of Adjustments;
6. To leave on the premises, free of encumbrance and fully paid for, chattels and fixtures included in this transaction as listed in Agreement of Purchase and Sale herein;
7. To deliver up vacant possession and keys on closing.

Dated at   this day of   19 .

_____

This is a standard client's undertaking and may be adjusted according to the requirements of the particular transaction.

STATUTORY DECLARATION	) IN THE MATTER OF title to Lot
	) Plan , City of
PROVINCE OF ONTARIO	) Municipality of
	) municipally known as
JUDICIAL DISTRICT	)
OF YORK	)
	) AND IN THE MATTER OF the
	) sale thereof
	) FROM:
TO WIT:	) TO:

We,   and   , both of the City of
in the   of

SOLEMNLY DECLARE AS FOLLOWS:

1. That we are the Vendors with respect to the subject transaction and as such have personal knowledge of the matters hereinafter deposed to;
2. That we are not, and will not be at the time of the conveyance of the Lands, non-residents of Canada within the meaning of Section 116 of the Income Tax Act of Canada, as amended;
3. That we are spouses of one another and we have each attained the age of eighteen years;
4. That to the best of our knowledge and belief, the subject conveyance does not contravene section 49 of the Planning Act, 1983.

AND we make this solemn Declaration, conscientiously believing it to be true and knowing that it is of the same force and effect as if made under oath and by virtue of the Canada Evidence Act.

SEVERALLY sworn before me at   )
the City of Toronto, in the   )
Municipality   )
of Metropolitan Toronto, this   )   _____
day of   , 19 .)
)
)
)   _____
)

A Commissioner, etc.

To:

And to: Barrister and Solicitor

Re: Sale to

DIRECTION

We hereby authorize and direct you to make the balance due on closing with respect to the above-noted transaction in favour of our solicitors,
                    IN TRUST, or as they may in writing, direct and for so doing this shall be your good and sufficient authority.

BILL OF SALE

We hereby transfer and convey to the purchaser the chattels, fixtures and additional items included in this transaction as listed in the Agreement of Purchase and Sale and we covenant that we are the lawful owners thereof and that there are no liens, encumbrances or claims affecting the same, and that we have the right to transfer and convey the same.

WARRANTY

We hereby warrant that the dwellings situate on the above-noted lands are not, and never have been, insulated with urea formaldehyde foam insulation, which warranty shall survive the closing of the transaction and not merge on same.

DATED at   this   day of   , 19 .

_____

TENDER

To make tender is to provide evidence that you are ready to close the transaction when the solicitor on the other side is not. A witness should be present. All the documents necessary to effect a closing are exchanged just as on a closing. Check the Affidavit of Residence and of Value of the Consideration, the affidavit of execution, and the description of the lands. The documents must be in registrable form. On completion they are returned to their respective owners and tender has been effected.

Part V

THE LAND REGISTRATION REFORM
ACT, 1984

CHAPTER 14

THE LAND REGISTRATION REFORM ACT, 1984

By now the Land Registration Reform Act, 1984, S.O. 1984, c. 32, needs no introduction. It was legislated to advance the Province of Ontario Land Registration System, POLARIS, the automated system designed to store title records in individual computer indexes. It became effective on April 1, 1985, O. Reg. 35/38, and is under way in several land registration offices, but conversion of the entire province will take considerable time.

The new document forms provided under Part I of the Act have been explained in the relevant chapters of this book. They were intended to accommodate the microfilming process, and at the same time to provide the information required for registration purposes.

Part II relates to designation of properties to POLARIS and provides the following:

1. a computerized version of title records, formerly recorded in abstract books and parcel registers, and
2. a property mapping system on which all lands designated to the system are indicated and assigned a property identification number — PIN.

TITLE SEARCH

Under the Land Titles system the entries on the current parcel register are loaded into the computer under the PIN assigned the particular parcel. They include:

1. the designation date;
2. the land description, parcel and section, and
3. the registered owner and all encumbrances.

On activating the computer with the PIN, a printout of the title just loaded may be retrieved. Updating (subsearching) is possible as documents are registered.

Under the Registry system, designated properties are also assigned a PIN. A search of the abstract book from the last registered owner to the designation date is required and details of the documents are loaded into the computer. The process is referred to as parcelization.

To establish whether or not encumbrances were registered prior to the designation date, it is necessary to execute a 40-year manual search of the property. The parcelization staff do not check prior to the date of the last transfer/deed. The following information is loaded into the computer and retrieved on a printout:

1. designation date;
2. land description, and
3. the owner in the last registered transfer/deed, and subsequently, registered encumbrances only.

Documents may be reviewed on a microfilm fiche under both systems, and the original is available as in the past under the Registry system.

PROPERTY MAPPING

This provides a series of maps compiled for reference to properties designated for POLARIS. The counties are divided into blocks and Block Index Maps are compiled therefrom. Subsequently, they are divided into Property Index Maps from which you can determine the location of the property you wish to search. Lots on plans of subdivision and on concession lots are readily identified, also the property identification number.

PROPERTY IDENTIFICATION NUMBER

The method of procedure for identifying properties for title purposes does not relate to the traditional reference — lot and plan, and parcel and register numbers.

A five digit identification number, 00085, is assigned each block and given prominence in bold type on the Block Index Map. The block number for a particular property may be obtained from the Plan Index Map at the map counter. The properties within a block are indicated on the Property Index Map sheets. It is easy to pinpoint the plan of subdivision of interest to you, then the exact lot and abutting lands. Each lot is assigned a four digit number, 0027, and it is also indicated in bold type on the plan.

The five digit number, 00085, followed by the four digit number, 0027, make up the property identification number, 000850027 — a number unique to each property. It is the identification required to activate the computer terminal for loading information from registered documents and for retrieving a printout of the title.

There are alternatives for finding the PIN — the registration number of a document, a person's or corporation's name. They have limitations so it is usually faster to pursue the map index.

REGISTRATION OF DOCUMENTS

Prior to tendering a document for registration a printout should be obtained to establish the current status of the title. Then, observe the following:

1. the registration clerk activates the counter computer;
2. checks the land description and the registered owner displayed on the screen with the document tendered; if they are identical the document is accepted;
3. the document is stamped with the Land Registrar's stamp and registration number;
4. the fee is paid;
5. the stamped duplicate document is returned to the person who tendered it, and
6. particulars from the document are typed on the keyboard and subsequently displayed on the screen.

CONDOMINIUMS

Property lines for condominium projects are not indicated on the property maps. The project is given a block number, 00096, plus the Condominium Plan number, 678. A reference index for the unit PIN is provided at the condominium service counter.

DOWNTIME PERIOD

Title searchers will be advised if downtime periods in the system will delay procedure sufficiently to refer to the manual back-up system. It includes the following:

1. property index books organized by the PIN which contain a record of registrations for each property, and
2. a list of registered documents.

PART III OF THE L.R.R.A., 1984

When it is introduced, further amendments to the Registry, Land Titles and Condominium Acts will be provided to accommodate the legislation brought into practice under Parts I and II.

APPENDICES

Appendix 1

CONVERSION OF IMPERIAL TO METRIC

The following are the *conversion factors* by which the number of imperial units is to be *multiplied* in order to obtain the S.I. equivalent.

LENGTH:

1 chain (66 feet)	=	20.116 8 m
1 foot	=	0.304 8 m
1 inch	=	0.025 4 m
1 mile	=	1.609 344 km
1 mile	=	1 609.344 m
1 perch	=	5.029 2 m
1 pole	=	5.029 2 m
1 rod	=	5.029 2 m
1 yard	=	0.914 4 m

AREA:

1 acre	=	4 046.856 m²
1 acre	=	0.404 685 6 ha
1 square foot	=	0.092 903 04 m²
1 square mile	=	2.589 988 km²
1 square yard	=	0.836 127 4 m²

In order to convert from S.I. units to imperial units the only step necessary is to *divide* the number of S.I. units by the conversion factors given above.

APPENDIX 2

METRIC LINEAR UNITS MOST FREQUENTLY USED

UNITS OF LENGTH

Metric linear units most frequently used:

> millimetre   (mm)
> centimetre   (cm)
> metre   (m)
> kilometre   (km)

The relationships between these four linear units are:

> 1 cm = 10 mm
> 1 m = 100 cm =1 000 mm
> 1 km = 1 000 m

ON METRIC PLANS OF SURVEY AND IN DESCRIPTIONS THE *METRE* (m) AND DECIMALS THEREOF ARE USED EXCLUSIVELY TO EXPRESS DISTANCES, EXCEPT FOR THE OCCASIONAL USE OF THE KILOMETRE (km) ON KEY PLANS.

UNITS OF AREA

The following units of area will be commonly used:

> square centimetre (cm^2)
> square metre (m^2)
> hectare   (ha)
> square kilometre (km^2)

The relationships between these units are:

> $1 m^2$ = 10 000 cm^2
> 1 ha = 10 000 m^2
> $1 km^2$ = 100 ha

APPENDIX 3

SURVEYORS' MEASURE

7.92 inches	= 1 link
25 links	= 1 rod, pole or perch
	(all of equal length)
100 links)	= 1 chain
)	= 4 rods
80 chains	= 1 mile
625 square links	= 1 square rod
16 square rods	= 1 square chain
10 square chains	= 1 acre
43,560 square feet	= 1 acre
1 chain	= 66 feet

Appendix 4

SIGNIFICANT DATES
(AFFIDAVITS, CONSENTS, *ETC.*)

1921 June 1	Land Transfer Tax affidavit.
1922 June 13	Impossible to acquire prescriptive title against municipal roads after this date. (Limitations Act s. 16.)
1929 June 1	Affidavit of Celibacy.
1937 January 1	All documents perforated "registered".
1939 June 25	Affidavit of Age and Marital Status in Deed or Mortgage when wife joins to bar dower.
1941 April 9	Affidavit of Marital Status.
1954 April 30	Affidavit of Mortmain. (Ontario companies exempt June 23/65. Quebec companies exempt January 1/69.)
1952 January 1	Old Age Pensions Assistance Act repealed.
1957 April 1	Affidavit of Age: Men and Women (except joint tenants) on Deed and Mortgage. Affidavit of Marital Status: Men, if no-one joins in Deed or Mortgage as wife.
1958 March 1	Affidavit of Age: All Grantors except Executor, Administrator, Trustee under Will or Public Trustee.
1959 January 1	Dominion Estate Tax Consent (revoked January 1/72) Income Tax Act.
1959	Assets of Canadian Farm Loan Board vested in Farm Credit Corporation. Canada Statute.
1961 March 29	Planning Board Consent.
1964 May 8	Retail Sales Tax Clearance (repealed April/76).
1964 July 1	Affidavit of Age in Powers of Attorney, Leases, Assignments of Lease and Mortgages. Affidavit of Marital Status made by man or wife. At least one given name to be shown for Grantees other than corporations.
1965 May 3	Power of granting Planning Act (s. 29) consents transferred from Planning Board to Committee of Adjustment, Land Division Committees or Department of Municipal Affairs (Planning Amendment Act, 1964, S.O. 1964, c. 90).
1965 June 23	No Affidavit of Mortmain for Ontario companies.
1967 January 1	Affidavit of Age on Discharges of Mortgage.
1967 January 1	Deed to uses — legislation.

1967 June 1	Planning Act — remedial legislation.
1967 June 15	Violations of Planning Act s. 29 forgiven prior to this date. (Planning Amendment Act, 1967, S.O. 1967, c. 75, s. 10(3).)
1968 January 1	Capacity of Officer signing for Corporation.
1968 May 3	Parcels of more than 10 acres no longer exempt from Planning Act s. 29. (Planning Amendment Act, 1968, S.O. 1968, c. 96.)
1969 May 13	Affidavit of marital status any time wife joins.
1970 January 1	Succession duty consent for estates (revoked April 10/79).
1970 June 27	Subdivision and Part-Lot Control throughout Ontario.
1971 September 1	Age of majority changed to 18 from 21.
1972 January 1	Affidavit of Residence. (Income Tax Act (Canada) s. 116.)
1973 January 1	All new plans of subdivision registered land titles.
1973 April 1	Reference Plans required for all severances.
1973 July 1	Tax Certificates under Municipal Affairs Act (covers Scarborough), and conveyances under Assessment Act and Municipal Act confirmed to this date. Tax Sales Confirmation Act (1974).
1973 August 1	Registration of Notice, or Assignment of Agreement of Purchase and Sale, or Option to Purchase valid for one year.
1974 January 1	West Rouge annexed by Scarborough.
1974 January 9	Severance not required when mortgage held on adjoining land.
1974 April 10	Affidavit of Residence by purchaser inserted in deed.
1974 April 10	Land Speculation Tax affidavit or Clearance stamp (repealed October 24/78).
1977 July 12	Succession Duty Release not required for Discharges of Mortgage.
1978 January 19	Succession Duty Release not required for documents by surviving joint tenant, affidavit should explain. (Succession Duty Act, O. Reg. 44/78.)
1978 March 31	Family Law Reform Act, 1978, S.O. 1978, c. 2, s. 70. Abolished dower, except where previously vested, created right of posession to spouse in matrimonial home.
1979 March 31	Consent to severance once granted not required again — a search behind Consent for compliance not necessary. Not retroactive. (Planning Act s. 29(4b) and (4d).)

1979 November 30	Corporation Tax Lien effective only if registered on title.
	Corporations Tax Act, 1972, S.O. 1972, c. 143, s. 167 repealed.
1980 January 1	No claim against land for Mortgage if discharge registered more than ten years. Nor for *Lis Pendens* Construction Lien, or Certificate of Action, Notice of Conditional Sale, Gas or Oil Lease or Notice of Security Interest if discharge has been registered more than two years. (Registry Act s. 65(1).)
1981 June 26	Consent Planning Act for partition orders (s. 49(20)).
1982 June 15	Mortmain and Charitable Uses Act repealed.
1983 April 2	Construction Lien Act, S.O. 1983, c. 6, in force.
1983 August 1	Planning Act, 1983, S.O. 1983, c. 1, provided an exemption for a grant or remaining parcel where consent obtained to convey abutting parcel (s. 49(6).)
1984 November 1	Part I of L.R.R.A., 1984 introduced in Oxford County. All affidavits except residence and value of the consideration replaced with statements. Where statements signed, the conveyance and all prior conveyances deemed to comply with s. 49 of Planning Act, 1983 and predecessors.
	Second given name of purchaser required.
1985 January 1	Part I of L.R.R.A. 1984 introduced in all Ontario.
1986 March 1	Family Law Reform Act, R.S.O. 1980, c. 152 renamed Dower and Miscellaneous Abolition Act (Family Law Act, S.O. 1986, c. 4, s. 71(4).)
1988 March 31	Vested dower rights abolished unless notice of claim registered.

APPENDIX 5

LAND REGISTRY OFFICES (April 1990)

DIVISION	LAND REGISTRAR	ADDRESS	TELEPHONE
Algoma No. 1 (Reg. & L.T.)	Penny Hanson (Mrs.)	P.O. Box 550, 520 Queen St. East *Sault Ste. Marie.* P6A 5M8	(705) 253-8887 PUBLIC—(705) 253-9151
Brant No. 2 (Reg.)	P. Gale (Mrs.)	Court House, 80 Wellington Street, *Brantford.* N3T 2L9	(519) 752-8321
Bruce No. 3 (Reg. & L.T.)	Lee Trevors (Acting)	203 Cayley Street, P.O. Box 1690, *Walkerton.* N0G 2V0	(519) 881-2251 881-2259
Ottawa-Carleton No. 4 (L.T.)	J.H. Hale	Court House, 161 Elgin St. 4th Floor, *Ottawa.* K2P 2K1	(613) 239-1230

The Land Titles Division of Ottawa-Carleton No. 4 includes all of the Regional Municipality of Ottawa-Carleton except the Township of Cumberland.

Ottawa-Carleton No. 5 (Reg.)	D.P. Potterton	Court House, 4th Floor, 161 Elgin Street, *Ottawa.* K1N 7B9	(613) 239-1319

The Registry Division of Ottawa-Carleton No. 5 includes all of the Regional Municipality of Ottawa-Carleton except the Township of Cumberland.

Cochrane No. 6 (Reg. & L.T.)	T. Miedema	Court House, 149 4th Avenue, P.O. Box 580, *Cochrane.* P0L 1C0	(705) 272-5791

The geographic townships of Ben Nevis, Benoit, Bisley, Pontiac, Keefer, Clifford, McEvay, Timmins and Tolstoi, in the Territorial District of Cochrane, remain in the Registry and Land Titles Divisions of Temiskaming.

Dufferin No. 7 (Reg.)	J.A. Crawford (Mrs.)	10 Louisa Street, *Orangeville.* L9W 3P9	(519) 941-1481
Dundas No. 8 (Reg.)	Dennis Hinz	5th Street, *Morrisburg.* K0C 1X0	(613) 543-2583

DIVISION	LAND REGISTRAR	ADDRESS	TELEPHONE
Port Hope No. 9 (Reg. & L.T.)	Pauline Green (Ms.)	17 Mill St. North, P.O. Box 122, *Port Hope.* L1A 3W3	(416) 885-5616

The Land Titles Division of Port Hope No. 9 includes the Town of Port Hope and the Township of Hope in the County of Northumberland, the Village of Millbrook and the Township of Cavan in the County of Peterborough, and the Township of Manvers in the County of Victoria. The Registry Division of Port Hope No. 9 includes parts only of the Town of Port Hope (the remainder is in the Registry Division of Northumberland West No. 39) but otherwise it is coextensive with the Land Titles Division of Port Hope No. 9.

Newcastle No. 10 (Reg. & L.T.)	Janet Price (Ms.)	108 Liberty St. North, P.O. Box 178, *Bowmanville.* L1C 3K9	(416) 623-5386

The Registry and Land Titles Divisions of Newcastle No. 10 include the Town of Newcastle (which consists of the former townships of Clarke and Darlington, the former Town of Bowmanville and the former Village of Newcastle, in the County of Durham), and that part of the Township of Scugog that was formerly the Township of Cartwright in the County of Durham.

Elgin No. 11 (Reg. & L.T.)	William W. Burke	Wellington Street, P.O. Box 4, *St. Thomas.* N5P 3T5	(519) 631-3015

The Land Titles Division of Kent (Lake Erie) is combined with the office for the registry system for the County of Elgin and R.H. Davis is the Land Registrar.

Essex No. 12 (Reg. & L.T.)	Wayne W. Patterson	250 Windsor Avenue, 3rd Floor, *Windsor.* N9A 6P8	(519) 971-9980 PUBLIC—(519) 256-4996

Frontenac No. 13 (Reg.)	W.D. Robertson	Court House, *Kingston.* K7L 2N4	(613) 548-6767 PUBLIC—(613) 542-1783

Glengarry No. 14 (Reg.)	Jean Claude Brisson	P.O. Box 668, 63 Kenyon Street West, *Alexandria.* K0C 1A0	(613) 525-1315

Grenville No. 15 (Reg. & L.T.)	L.A. Cross	499 Centre Street, P.O. Box 1660, *Prescott.* K0E 1T0	(613) 925-3177

DIVISION	LAND REGISTRAR	ADDRESS	TELEPHONE

The Land Titles Division of Grenville No. 15 consists only of parts of the Township of Edwardsburgh.

Grey North *No. 16* (Reg.)	Paul Nixon	Court House, 595 9th Avenue East, *Owen Sound.* N4K 3E3	(519) 376-1637 PUBLIC—(519) 376-1647

The Registry Division of Grey North No. 16 includes the City of Owen Sound, the towns of Meaford and Thornbury, the Villages of Chatsworth and Shallow Lake, and the Townships of Collingwood, Derby, Euphrasia, Holland, Keppel, St. Vincent, Sarawak, Sullivan and Sydenham.

Grey South *No. 17* (Reg.)	Paul Nixon	192 Lambton Street East, P.O. Box 10, *Durham.* N0G 1R0	(519) 369-2011

The Registry Division of Grey South No. 17 includes the Towns of Durham and Hanover, the Villages of Dundalk, Flesherton, Markdale and Neustadt, and the Townships of Artemesia, Bentinck, Egremont, Glenelg, Normanby, Osprey and Proton. Mount Forest is in Wellington County.

Haldimand *No. 18* (Reg.)	Norma J. Davidson	P.O. Box 310, 10 Echo Street, *Cayuga.* N0A 1E0	(416) 772-3531

Haliburton *No. 19* (Reg.)	Melvin L. Flood	P.O. Box 270, Newcastle Street, *Minden.* K0M 2K0	(705) 286-1391

Halton No. 20 (Reg. L.T.)	John Menard	491 Steeles Avenue East, *Milton.* L9T 1Y7	(416) 878-7287 (416) 878-8159 PUBLIC

The Registry and Land Titles Divisions of Halton No. 20 include all of the former County of Halton, except that part of the Township of Nassagaweya which was annexed to the Township of Eramosa in the County of Wellington and part of the Town of Oakville which was annexed to the City of Mississauga in the Regional Municipality of Peel.

Hastings No. 21 (Reg. & L.T.)	S.C. Geneja	280 Pinnacle Street, *Belleville.* K8N 3B1	(613) 968-4597

Huron No. 22 (Reg.)	D.G. Hill Patricia E. MacLean	38 North Street, P.O. Box 216, *Goderich.* N7A 3Z2	(519) 524-9562

Kenora No. 23 (Reg. & L.T.)	R. Edmonds Linda McGeachy	220 Main Street South, P.O. Box 1350, *Kenora.* P9N 3X7	(807) 468-3138

DIVISION	LAND REGISTRAR	ADDRESS	TELEPHONE
Kent No. 24 (Reg.)	D.R. Craven Ray Reeson	40 William Street North, *Chatham.* N7M 5L8	(519) 352-5520
Kent (Lake Erie) (L.T.) See *Elgin No. 11*	R.H. Davis William W. Burke	Wellington Street, P.O. Box 4, *St. Thomas.* N5P 3T5	(519) 631-3015

The office for the Land Titles Division of Kent (Lake Erie) is combined with the office for the registry system for the County of Elgin.

Lambton No. 25 Reg.)	K. Doan	Court House, 700 N. Christina Street, P.O. Box 3021, *Sarnia.* N7T 7N5	(519) 337-2393 Ext. 40
Lanark North No. 26 (Reg.)	J.C. Smithson Desmond Dias	125 Brougham Street, P.O. Box 1180, *Almonte.* K0A 1A0	(613) 256-1577

The Registry Division of Lanark North No. 26 includes the Town of Almonte and part of the Town of Carleton Place (excluding part annexed from the Township of Beckwith, which is in the Registry Division of Lanark South No. 27), the Village of Lanark and the Townships of Dalhousi, Darling, Lanark, Lavant, North Sherbrooke, Pakenham and Ramsay.

Lanark South No. 27 (Reg.)	D.T. Wilson	10 Sunset Blvd., P.O. Box 278, *Perth.* K7H 3E4	(613) 267-1144

The Registry Division of Lanark South No. 27 includes the Towns of Perth and Smiths Falls, and part of the Town of Carleton Place that was formerly part of the Township of Beckwith, and the Townships of Bathurst, Beckwith, Drummond, Montague, North Burgess, North Elmsley and South Sherbrooke.

Leeds No. 28 (Reg.)	L.A. Cross	P.O. Box 146, 7 King Street West, *Brockville.* K6V 5V2	(613) 345-5751
Lennox No. 29 (Reg.)	B.M. Drew	87 Thomas Street, P.O. Box 459, *Napanee.* K0K 2R0	(613) 354-3751
Manitoulin No. 31 (Reg. & L.T.)	J.A. Graham Ron J. Lane	Phipps Street, P.O. Box 265, *Gore Bay.* P0P 1H0	(705) 282-2442
Middlesex East No. 33 (Reg. & L.T.)	R.K. Nuijten Larry Dalton	80 Dundas Street, P.O. Box 5600, *London.* N6A 2P3	(519) 675-7600 (519) 679-7190 PUBLIC

DIVISION	LAND REGISTRAR	ADDRESS	TELEPHONE

The Registry and Land Titles Divisions of Middlesex East No. 33 include the City of London, the Town of Parkhill, the Villages of Ailsa Craig and Lucan, the Townships of Adelaide, Biddulph, East Williams, Lobo, London, McGillivray, North Dorchester, West Nissouri, Westminister and West Williams.

| *Middlesex West* No. 34 (Reg. & L.T.) | W.S. Newman | 178 McKellar Street, P.O. Drawer 9, *Glencoe.* N0L 1M0 | (519) 287-2234 |

The Registry and Land Titles Divisions of Middlesex West No. 34 include the Town of Strathroy, the Villages of Glencoe, Newbury and Wardsville, and the Townships of Caradoc, Delaware, Ekfrid, Metcalfe and Mosa.

Muskoka No. 35 (Reg. & L.T.)	R.C. Stewart	15 Dominion Street, P.O. Box 720, *Bracebridge.* P0B 1C0	(705) 645-4415
Niagara North No. 30 (Reg. & L.T.)	John P. Grammar	59 Church Street, P.O. Box 126, *St. Catharines.* L2R 6R4	(416) 684-6351
Niagara South No. 59 (Reg. & L.T.)	Dave Hill	200 Division Street, *Welland.* L3B 3G1	(416) 735-4011-13
Nipissing No. 36 (Reg. & L.T.)	Rodney C. Wickett (Acting)	360 Plouffe Street, *North Bay.* P1B 9L5	(705) 474-2270
Norfolk No. 37 (Reg.)	Norma Davidson	Court House, #3 Highway West, *Simcoe.* N3Y 4K8	(519) 426-2216
Haldimand-Norfolk (37) (L.T.)	Norma Davidson	Court House, #3 Highway West, *Simcoe.* N3Y 4K8	(519) 426-2216

The Land Titles Division of Haldimand-Norfolk No. 37 includes the City of Nanticoke, the Town of Haldimand and the Town of Dunnville as described in Schedules 9 and 10, 11 and 12, and 13, respectively, to O. Reg. 69/77; and the former Land Titles Divisions of Haldimand (Lake Erie) and Norfolk (Land Erie) as constituted by O. Reg. 254/73.

| *Northumberland East (38)* (Reg.) | Doreen Snider | 51 King Street East, P.O. Box 339, *Colborne.* K0K 1S0 | (416) 355-2338 |

The Registry Division of Northumberland East No. 38 includes the Town of Campbellford, the Villages of Brighton, Colborne and Hastings, and the Townships of Brighton, Cramahe, Murray, Percy and Seymour.

DIVISION	LAND REGISTRAR	ADDRESS	TELEPHONE
Northumberland West (39) (Reg.)	Pauline Green	P.O. Box 668, 1005 William Street, Suite 105, *Cobourg.* K9A 4R5	(416) 372-3813

The Registry Division of Northumberland West No. 39 includes the Town of Cobourg, part of the Town of Port Hope, and the Townships of Alnwick, Haldimand, and Hamilton; and the Township of South Monaghan in the County of Peterborough, formerly in the County of Northumberland.

Durham No. 40 (Reg. & L.T.)	Terry Brown	850 King Street West, *Whitby.* L1J 2L5	(416) 436-3521

The Registry and Land Titles Divisions of Durham No. 40 include all that part of the Regional Municipality of Durham consisting of the former County of Ontario except the Townships of Rama and Mara annexed to the County of Simcoe and part of the Township of Pickering annexed to the Borough of Scarborough in the Municipality of Metropolitan Toronto.

Oxford No. 41 (Reg. & L.T.)	R.K. Thompson	75 Graham Street, P.O. Box 246, *Woodstock.* N4S 7W8	(519) 537-6287
Parry Sound No. 42 (Reg. & L.T.)	J.M. Boyer	28 Miller Street, P.O. Box 276, *Parry Sound.* P2A 2X4	(705) 746-5816
Peel No. 43 (Reg. & L.T.)	D.O. Cannon, Q.C. Al Cordery	7765 Hurontario Street, P.O. Box 1200, *Brampton.* L6V 2L8	(416) 457-5350 (416) 457-5610 PUBLIC

The Registry and Land Titles Divisions of Peel No. 43 include all of the Regional Municipality of Peel consisting of the former County of Peel and part of the Town of Oakville in the former County of Halton, now part of the City of Mississauga.
Note: There is no long distance charge for telephone calls from Toronto.

Perth No. 44 (Reg.)	Grace E. Park (Acting)	York Street West, P.O. Box 902, *Stratford.* N5A 6T1	(519) 271-3343
Peterborough No. 45 (Reg. & L.T.)	Robert Appleton	Court House, 470 Water Street, *Peterborough.* K9H 3M3	(705) 745-0583

The Registry and Land Titles Divisions of Peterborough No. 45 include all of the County of Peterborough except the Townships of Cavan and South Monaghan and the Village of Millbrook which remain in the Registry and Land Titles Divisions of Port Hope No. 9.

DIVISION	LAND REGISTRAR	ADDRESS	TELEPHONE
Prescott No. 46 (Reg. & L.T.)	Louis Arki	Queen & Court Sts., P.O. Box 302, *L'Original.* K0B 1K0	(613) 675-4648
Prince Edward No. 47 (Reg.)	R.G. Rowe	P.O. Box 1310, 1 Pitt Street, *Picton.* K0K 2T0	(613) 476-3219
Rainy River No. 48 (Reg. & L.T.)	R. Bibby	353 Church Street, P.O. Box 398, *Fort Frances.* P6A 3M7	(807) 274-5451
Renfrew No. 49 (Reg.)	Robert Price	400 Pembroke Street East, P.O. Box 760, *Pembroke.* K8A 6X1	(613) 732-8331
Russell No. 50 (Reg. & L.T.)	Roland Gregoire	469 Concession Street, P.O. Box 10, *Russell.* K0A 3B0	(613) 445-2138

The Registry and Land Titles Divisions of Russell No. 50 include the Town of Rockland, the Village of Casselman, and the Townships of Cambridge, Clarence and Russell; and the Township of Cumberland in the Regional Municipality of Ottawa-Carleton.

Simcoe No. 51 (Reg. & L.T.)	William Broadhurst	Court House, 114 Worsley Street, *Barrie.* L4M 1M1	(705) 734-2722 PUBLIC—(705) 737-3600

The Registry and Land Titles Divisions of Simcoe No. 51 consist of the whole of the County of Simcoe including the Townships of Rama and Mara annexed from the former County of Ontario.

Stormont No. 52 (Reg.)	M. Lois Comrie (Mrs.)	P.O. Box 1268, 127 Sydney Street, *Cornwall.* K6H 5V3	(613) 932-4522
Sudbury No. 53 (Reg. & L.T.)	Arvind Damley (Acting)	199 Larch St., 3rd Floor, *Sudbury.* P3E 4S7	(705) 675-4300 Exts. 244, 245
Temiskaming No. 54 (Reg. & L.T.)	Lorraine Leblanc	375 Main Street, P.O. Box 159, *Haileybury.* P0J 1P0	(705) 672-3332

DIVISION	LAND REGISTRAR	ADDRESS	TELEPHONE

The geographic Townships of Ben Nevis, Benoit, Bisley, Pontiac, Keefer, Clifford, McEvay, Timmins and Tolstoi, in the Territorial District of Cochrane, remain in the Registry and Land Titles Division of Temiskaming.

Thunder Bay No. 55 (Reg. & L.T.)	Robert Johnson	29 Royston Court, Postal Station "P", *Thunder Bay.* P7A 4Y7	(807) 475-1235 PUBLIC—(807) 345-0553
Toronto No. 63 (Reg.)	J. Haughey	230-20 Dundas St. West, 2nd Floor *Toronto.* M5G 2C2	(416) 965-7553 PUBLIC — (416) 965-7546

The Registry Division of Toronto No. 63 includes the whole of the City of Toronto.

Toronto Borough No. 64 (Reg.)	David Thompson	321-20 Dundas St. West 3rd Floor *Toronto.* M5G 2C2	(416) 965-7588 PUBLIC—(416) 965-7601

The Registry Division of Toronto Boroughs & York South No. 64 consists of all of the Municipality of Metropolitan Toronto, except the City of Toronto, including the boroughs of York, East York, North York, Etobicoke and Scarborough and part of the Township of Pickering in the former County of Ontario annexed to the Borough of Scarborough; and the part of the Regional Municipality of York, including the Town of Markham and parts of the Towns of Richmond Hill, Vaughan and Whitchurch-Stouffville included in the former Townships of Vaughan and Markham prior to January 1, 1971.

Metropolitan Toronto No. 66 (L.T.)	John R. Hayward	420-20 Dundas St. West, 4th Floor *Toronto.* M5G 2C2	(416) 965-5248 PUBLIC—(416) 965-7611 Condominium — PUBLIC—(416) 965-7614

The Land Titles Division of Toronto and York South No. 66 includes The Municipality of Metropolitan Toronto and that part of The Regional Municipality of York that, together, are included in the Registry Divisions of Toronto and Toronto Boroughs and York South.

Victoria No. 57 (Reg.)	E. A. Legacy	Provincial Court Building 440 Kent St. West, P.O. Box 430, *Lindsay.* K9V 4S5	(705) 324-4912

The Registry Division of Victoria No. 57 includes all of the County of Victoria, except the Township of Manvers which remains in the Registry and Land Titles Division of Port Hope No. 9.

Waterloo North No. 58 (Reg.)	Murray Smith	200 Frederick Street, 3rd Floor, *Kitchener.* N2G 3W9	(519) 576-1330 PUBLIC—(519)576-6600

DIVISION	LAND REGISTRAR	ADDRESS	TELEPHONE

The Registry Division of Waterloo North No. 58 includes that part of the City of Cambridge lying north of the northern limits of concessions IV, III, II and I of the former Township of Waterloo and north of the northern limit of Beasley's Broken Front Concession of the said former Township and the production thereof to the centre thread of the Grand River, the Cities of Kitchener and Waterloo, and the Townships of Wellesley, Wilmot and Woolwich.

Waterloo South	Margaret Wiseman	99 Main Street,	(519) 653-5778
No. 67		(The Mall)	
(Reg.)		*Cambridge.*	
		N1R 1W1	

The Registry Division of Waterloo South No. 67 includes all that part of the City of Cambridge lying south of the northern limits of concessions IV, III, II and I of the former Township of Waterloo and south of the northern limit of Beasley's Broken Front Concession of the said former Township and the production thereof to the centre thread of the Grand River, and the Township of North Dumfries, including part of Beverly Township in the former County of Wentworth, annexed to the said Registry Division by O. Reg. 154/73.

Wellington North	Brenda Quaranto	248 George Street,	(519) 848-2300
No. 60		P.O. Box 389,	
(Reg.)		*Arthur.*	
		N0G 1A0	

The Registry Division of Wellington North No. 60 includes the Towns of Harriston, Mount Forest and Palmerston, the Villages of Arthur, Clifford and Drayton, and the Townships of Arthur, Maryborough, Minto, Peel, West Garagraxa, and West Luther.

Wellington South	A.G. Sharp	P.O. Box 905,	(519) 822-0251
No. 61		21 Douglas Street,	
(Reg.)		*Guelph.*	
		N1H 6M6	

The Registry Division of Wellington South No. 61 includes the City of Guelph, the Town of Fergus, the Villages of Elora and Erin, and the Townships of Eramosa, Erin, Guelph, Nichol, Pilkington with Puslinch.

Wentworth	Mrs. V. Mattuzzi	119 King St. West,	(416) 521-7561
No. 62		P.O. Box 2112,	PUBLIC—(416) 525-4571
(Reg. & L.T.)		*Hamilton.*	
		L8N 3Z9	

The Registry and Land Titles Divisions of Wentworth No. 62 consist of all of the Regional Municipality of Hamilton-Wentworth, including the City of Hamilton, the Towns of Dundas (formerly the Town of Dundas and parts of the Townships of Ancaster and West Flamborough), Ancaster (formerly part of the Township of Ancaster) and Stoney Creek (formerly the Town of Stoney Creek and Township of Saltfleet) and the Townships of Flamborough (formerly Townships of East Flamborough, Beverly and part of West Flamborough and Village of Waterdown) and Glanbrook (formerly the Townships of Binbrook and Glanford).

DIVISION	LAND REGISTRAR	ADDRESS	TELEPHONE
York North No. 65 (Reg. & L.T.)	J. A. Small	50 Eagle St. W., *Newmarket.* L3Y 6B1	895-1561 PUBLIC—(416) 895-9801

The Registry and Land Titles Divisions of York North No. 65 consist of the Towns of Aurora and Newmarket and parts of the Towns of Richmond Hill (formerly parts of the Townships of King and Whitchurch in the County of York), Vaughan (formerly part of the Township of King in the County of York) and Whitchurch-Stouffville (formerly part of the Village of Stouffville and part of the Township of Whitchurch in the County of York), and the Townships of East Gwillimbury, Georgina and King, and the Townships of Markham and Vaughan, formerly in the Registry and Land Titles Office in Toronto.

APPENDIX 6

SHERIFFS' OFFICES

COUNTY & JUDICIAL DISTRICT IN WHICH SITUATED	COUNTY TOWN (ADDRESS TO COUNTY COURT HOUSE)	SHERIFF
Algoma Dist.	Sault Ste. Marie, P6A 5M8	D. T. Anderson (705) 253-3261
Brant	Brantford, N3T 2L9	J. S. Canning (519) 752-5941
Bruce	Walkerton, N0G 2V0	C. Reidl (519) 881-1772
Cochrane Dist.	Cochrane, P0L 1C0	R. Lamarche (705) 272-4256
Dufferin	Orangeville, (51 Zina St.) L9W 1E5	S. T. Collyer (519) 941-4744
Durham	Whitby, L1N 5S4	M. Bain (416) 668-6808
Elgin	St. Thomas, N5P 3T9	R. L. Lake (519) 631-3530
Essex	Windsor, N9A 6N4	D. J. C. Montague (519) 252-7209
Frontenac	Kingston, K7L 2N4	A. J. Woodman (613) 548-3291
Grey	Owen Sound, N4K 3E3	R. Fenton (519) 376-7535
Haldimand	Cayuga, N0A 1E0	K. C. Bannister (416) 426-6550
Halton	Milton, L9T 1Y7	R. M. Sprowl (416) 878-7285
Hamilton-Wentworth	Hamilton, L8N 1E9	R. B. Violin (416) 522-1318
Hastings	Belleville, (235 Pinnacle St.) K8N 3A9	R. C. Coveney (613) 962-9106
Huron	Goderich, N7A 1M2	Vacant (519) 524-7322
Kenora Dist.	Kenora, P9N 1S4	P. Spalton (807) 468-6270
Kent	Chatham, N7M 4K1	G. D. B. Sulman (519) 352-7740
Lambton	Sarnia, N7T 7N5	S. Barber (519) 337-3265
Lanark	Perth, K7H 3E2	K. E. R. Fournier (613) 267-2021
Leeds & Grenville	Brockville, K6V 5T7	Helen Mick (613) 732-2541
Lennox & Addington	Napanee, K0K 2R0	Mrs. S. E. Valentyne (613) 354-3845
Manitoulin	Gore Bay, P0P 1H0	R. J. Lane (705) 282-2461
Middlesex	London, N6A 1E7	Robert Hawken (519) 679-7140
Muskoka Dist.	Bracebridge, P0B 1C0	C. Lynne Wagner (705) 645-8793
Niagara North (Judicial Dist. Of)	St. Catharines, (Box 465) L2R 6V9	P. Clark (416) 685-7341
Niagara South (Judicial Dist. Of)	Welland, L3B 3W6	L. E. Taylor (416) 734-6284
Nipissing Dist.	North Bay, P1B 4G1	Nestor Prisco
Norfolk	Simcoe, N3Y 4L2	K. C. Bannister (519) 426-6550
Northumberland	Cobourg, (Box 517) K9A 4L3	K. C. Gorman (416) 372-7812
Ottawa-Carleton (Judicial Dist. Of)	Ottawa, K1N 6E2	B. Hamilton (613) 238-1781
Oxford	Woodstock, N4S 7W5	R. S. Beaudoin (519) 539-6187
Parry Sound Dist.	Parry Sound, P2A 2X2	T. J. Healey (705) 746-2421

COUNTY & JUDICIAL DISTRICT IN WHICH SITUATED	COUNTY TOWN (ADDRESS TO COUNTY COURT HOUSE)	SHERIFF
Peel...................	Brampton, L6V 2M7	Vacant (416) 457-5400
Perth..................	Stratford, (Box 726) N5A 6V6	D. R. Misener (519) 271-1850
Peterborough...........	Peterborough, K9H 3M9	J. D. Lacombe (705) 745-0583
Prescott & Russell.......	L'Orignal, K0B 1K0	L. Cayen (613) 675-4567
Prince Edward..........	Picton, K0K 2T0	J. K. Maddox (613) 476-6236
Rainy River Dist.........	Fort Frances, P9A 3M7	J. E. Bradley (807) 274-5961
Renfrew...............	Pembroke,K8A 3K2	I. E. Schimmens (613) 732-2541
Simcoe................	Barrie, L4M 1M1	D. E. Edwards (705) 728-1221
Stormont, Dundas & Glengarry.............	Cornwall, (26 Pitt St.) K6J 3P2	J. A. R. Lamoureux (613) 932-1652
Sudbury Dist...........	Sudbury, P3C 1T9	A. Courjaud (705) 675-4158
Temiskaming Dist........	Haileybury, P0J 1K0	J.R. Dent (705) 672-3321
Thunder Bay Dist........	Thunder Bay, P7A 4B3	G. H. Burns (807) 475-1525
Victoria & Haliburton....	Lindsay, K9V 3R9	J. E. Boyd (705) 324-2542
Waterloo...............	Kitchener, N2H 1C3	Vacant (519) 742-1334
Wellington.............	Guelph, N1H 6J9	G. A. Goldrich (519) 824-4100
York Dist..............	Toronto, (361 University Ave.) M5G 1T4	B. C. Pitkin (416) 945-7491
York Region...........	Newmarket, (50 Eagle St. L3Y G5I)	G. A. Taggart (416) 853-4803

APPENDIX 7

SUGGESTED LIST OF REQUISITIONS UNDER THE REGISTRY ACT

1. Instrument No. 1732, page 3-Provincial Treasurer's Consent for Estate of James Rouse required;
2. Instrument No. 1834, page 4-Release of dower for Jane Craig;
3. Instrument No. 1991, page 6-Consent of Planning Board required;
4. Instrument No. 2834, page 9-Evidence that Tom Gibbon was a widower;
5. Instrument No. 2998, page 13-Evidence that agreement complied with;
6. Instrument No. 3421, page 21-Consent of Committee of Adjustment required — only part of land is mortgaged;
7. Instrument No. 3612, page 28-Registered owner John Jones to uses, agreement of purchase and sale signed by J. E. and Mary Jones.
8. Easement No. 2345-The agreement of purchase and sale does not recite that the lot is subject to this easement.
9. Notice of Conditional Sale No. 3485-with Consumers' gas for an air conditioner, the agreement of purchase and sale recites that the air conditioner is included in the purchase price so a discharge of said Notice is required.
10. Instrument No. 6754 is a grant of the subject lands to John Parks, subsequently Robert Parks conveyed the same land to Ann Koski, instrument No. 6999. There is a gap in the chain of title between the two conveyances and no evidence of a relationship between the Parks, nor is there a will registered for the estate of John Parks. We require a deed from John Parks to Robert Parks to feed the title or the will of John Parks wherein the subject land has been vested in Robert Parks free of claim of the beneficiaries.
11. Instrument No. 7788-Jo Troy purchased the whole of lot 8, Plan 60 and subsequently granted the east half to John Small, instrument No. 7888, and the west half to Jean Kelly, instrument No. 7889. The land was subject to the part lot control provisions of the Planning Act and amendments thereto. Neither grant indicates that consent was obtained from the Committee of Adjustment to sever the lot. They are in contravention of the Act and so title remains in the name of Jo Troy. Plan 60 was later exempted from the provisions of the Planning Act by By-Law No. 77889 making it possible for Jo Troy to deliver correcting deeds for the said half lots.
12. Instrument No. 8899 is a grant in favour of Arthur Investments

Limited. Arthur Investment Inc. subsequently granted to John Sarks. The corporate seal affixed to the instrument reads, Arthur Investments Limited. We require a correcting deed from Arthur Investments Limited to John Sarks.

There will be many more requisitions. These are merely the preliminaries which should alert searchers to the errors and omissions they may find along the way.

INDEX